The
Heritage
of American Catholicism

A TWENTY-EIGHT-VOLUME SERIES DOCUMENTING THE HISTORY
OF AMERICA'S LARGEST RELIGIOUS DENOMINATION

EDITED BY

Timothy Walch

ASSOCIATE EDITOR
U.S. Catholic Historian

A Garland Series

The Catholic Church and Human Rights

ITS ROLE IN THE FORMULATION OF U.S. POLICY
1945-1980

Jo Renee Formicola

Garland Publishing, Inc.
New York & London
1988

LIBRARY OF CONGRESS CATALOGING-IN-PUBLICATION DATA

Formicola, Jo Renee
   The Catholic Church and human rights : its role in the formulation of U. S. policy,
1945-1980 / Jo Renee Formicola.
    p. cm. — (The Heritage of American Catholicism)
   Revision of the author's thesis (Ph. D.—Drew University, 1981) originally presented
under the title; The Catholic Church and its role in the formulation of United States
human rights foreign policy, 1945-1978.
   Bibliography; p.
   ISBN 0-8240-4090-2 (alk. paper)
   1. Catholic Church—United States—Political activity—History—20th century.
2. Catholic Church. National Conference of Catholic Bishops—Political activity—
History—20th century.   3. Human rights—Religious aspects—Catholic Church—
History—20th century.   4. United States—Foreign relations—1945-   5. Church and
state—United States—History—20th century.   6. Lobbying—United States—History—
20th century. I. Title. II. Series.
BX1407.P63F66 1988
322'.1'0973—dc19   88-28693

DESIGN BY MARY BETH BRENNAN

PRINTED ON ACID-FREE, 250-YEAR-LIFE PAPER.
MANUFACTURED IN THE UNITED STATES OF AMERICA

Dedication

to Neal, my mentor and friend
to Allan, my husband and strongest supporter
to Matthew and Allison, my children who
    endured years without chocolate chip cookies

Contents

CHAPTER I: INTRODUCTION

On 25 October 1979, President Carter, speaking from the press room of the White House, announced a series of United States financial pledges to assist with Cambodian relief efforts "after meeting with a group of leaders of religious and other private organizations".[1] The New York Times covered the event and used it as its lead story. Also appearing on the front page was a picture of the President flanked by Terence Cardinal Cooke, Archbishop of New York, and the Reverend Theodore Hesburgh, President of Notre Dame University. Thirty-five years ago, that picture and what it represented, a cooperative effort between Church and State, initiated by influential members of the Catholic Church and supported by the United States Government, would have created a furor in some American circles. By 1979, no one seemed to notice. Yet, such events, as well as increased Church-State interaction, should stimulate academic inquiry by both political scientists and students of religion, for they lead us to ask the question: what impact does religion have on the development of public policy in the United States?

Literature on this topic is scarce. Gerhard Lenski, in 1963, tried to measure the consequences of religious beliefs on

---

[1]
Graham Hovey, "Carter Pledges Aid Up to $70 Million to Feed Cambodians", New York Times, 25 October 1979, p.1.

1

the economic and political values of American Jews, Catholics, and black and white Protestants in his classic sociological study, The Religious Factor.[2] Both Luke Ebersole in Church Lobbying in the Nation's Capital[3] and John L. Adams in The Growing Church Lobby in Washington,[4] attempted to explain as well as assess the activities and influence of various religious interest groups on a number of political issues. However, the most valuable study in the field continues to be an early work, Pressure Politics: The Story of the Anti-Saloon League written by Peter Odegard in 1928. It describes the efforts of a coalition of Protestant religious groups to influence the development of a public policy on one specific issue, temperance.[5]

This study is concerned with the endeavors of a particular religious institution, the American Catholic Church, and its efforts to work for the development of a more humane and moral foreign policy. For research and practical purposes, it is necessary to limit the term "American Catholic Church" to the

---

[2] Gerhard Lenski, The Religious Factor. A Sociological Study of Religion's Impact on Politics, Economics and Family Life, (New York: Doubleday, 1963).

[3] Luke Ebersole, Church Lobbying in the Nation's Capital, (New York: Macmillan, 1951).

[4] John L. Adams, The Growing Church Lobby in Washington, (Grand Rapids, Michigan: Wm. B. Eerdman's, 1970).

[5] Peter Odegard, Pressure Politics: The Story of the Anti-Saloon League, (New York: Octagon Books) 1966 edition. The denominations he discusses are essentially the Methodists, Baptists, Presbyterians and Congregationalists. See p. 18.

United States hierarchy, for that body alone makes American Catholic social and political policy for Church members through its regional, canonical organization, the National Conference of Catholic Bishops. Its central bureaucracy, the United States Catholic Conference, implements the foreign and domestic policies of the National Council of Catholic Bishops and carries out the daily work of the Church in religious as well as political, matters. Specifically, this book will focus on the issue of human rights, and will ask: what role did the American Catholic Church play in the formulation of U.S. human rights foreign policy from 1945 to 1980?

In this study, the term "human rights" will encompass those rights enumerated in the Universal Declaration of Human Rights of the United Nations, and those fundamental rights defined by the U.S. government, particularly during the Carter Administration.* Essentially, three classifications of inherent rights fall under the umbrella of international human rights: personal security rights, civil/political rights, and economic/welfare rights. The first category includes the right to be secure in one's person; to be free from torture, cruel and inhumane treatment, murder, kidnapping, arbitrary arrest, imprisonment or execution, with the right to a fair, prompt and public trial. The second category of civil/political rights

---

*
See particularly the address by Secretary of State Cyrus Vance, "Human Rights and Foreign Policy", Department of State Bulletin, May 23, 1977, pp. 505-507.

encompasses the right to free thought, speech, religion, press, movement, and participation in the government. The third category includes the right to vital needs, such as food, shelter, health care, and education.

The time span from 1945 to 1980 has been chosen for this study because it covers the era of heightened American concern for international human rights by both the U.S. government and the American Catholic Church. Within that same time frame, the American Catholic Church also evolved from an insignificant social and political force in the U.S., into an integral and potentially powerful interest group able to exert influence in the American political arena. With a following of approximately fifty million members,[6] the American Catholic Church now represents a special interest group larger than the membership of all U.S. labor unions combined![7]

However, the number of significant works on the subject of the American Catholic Church and its impact on U.S. public policy

---

[6] Felician A. Foy, gen.ed., 1978 Catholic Almanac,. (Huntington, Indiana: Our Sunday Visitor, 1978), p. 503. In 1977 there were 49,325,752 Catholics in the United States. This is 22.8% of the total U.S. population.

[7] U.S. Bureau of the Census, Statistical Abstracts of the United States,1978 (Washington: U.S. Government Printing Office, 1978), p. 430. In 1976 there were 25,486,000 members combined in AFL-CIO and other independent unions.

is brief. <u>American Catholics and the Roosevelt Presidency</u>[8] and
<u>Roosevelt and Romanism</u>,[9] by George Q. Flynn shed some light on
U.S. Catholic attitudes towards U.S. domestic and foreign policy
in the 1930's and 1940's. David O'Brien has contributed general
information to an understanding of Catholic involvement in
domestic policy in <u>American Catholics and Social Reform</u>,[10] as has
Donald Crosby in <u>God, Church and Flag</u>,[11] and Mary Hanna in
<u>Catholics and American Politics</u>.[12] Short of these works,
however, little else has been done to explicate the role of the
American Catholic Church in the formulation of either U.S.
domestic or foreign policy.

Hopefully, this book will help to fill that gap as it asks
the central question: what role did the American Catholic Church
play in the formulation of U.S. human rights foreign policy

8
George Q. Flynn, <u>American Catholics and the Roosevelt Presidency</u>, (Lexington: University of Kentucky Press, 1968).

9
George Q. Flynn, <u>Roosevelt and Romanism</u>, (Westport, Connecticut: Greenwood Press, 1976).

10
David O'Brien, <u>American Catholics and Social Reform</u>, (New York: Oxford University Press, 1968(.

11
Donald Crosby, <u>God, Church and Flag</u>, (Chapel Hill, North Carolina: University of North Carolina Press, 1978).

12
Mary Hanna, <u>Catholics and American Politics</u>, (Cambridge, Massachusetts: Harvard University Press, 1979).

between 1945 and 1980? Extensive research has led the author to conclude that the Church has played a positive but ever growing role in prodding the government to incorporate the principle of respect for human rights into U.S. foreign policy. This occurred gradually. Because the Church had little political influence during the post-War years (1945-1949), it played only a minor part in influencing U.S. human rights foreign policy, developing at that time. Later, during the Cold War years (1950-1965) and after, the Church became occupied with the problem of how to respond to Communism at home and abroad becoming complacent about international human rights. By the late 1960's, however, the American Catholic Church, socially and politically integrated into the American mainstream, and renewed by Vatican II, became involved in non-political attempts to bring to light reports of repression that it had been receiving from Latin America. The Church worked to inform and educate the public, the media, and the government about human rights abuses in the Southern Hemisphere. Finally, by the mid-1970's, the Church became involved politically, for the first time, on behalf of international human rights. It served as a credible witness before Congressional committees investigating human rights violations around the globe and supported, by lobbying, legislation which incorporated the principle of human rights into U.S. bilateral and multi-lateral foreign assistance. These efforts, however, were held to a modest level by factors that minimized the Church's effectiveness in the political arena: its commitment to a diverse number of interests, a lack of hierarchial support for human rights, its unique international position, and its uncertainty as to what political role, if any, the Church should play in the public policy debate. As those questions were resolved, in the 1980's, the Church went on to be the chief advocate of human rights in Latin America, and a major critic of the Reagan foreign policy posture in both El Salvador and Nicaragua.

Because this study dealt with a thirty five year time period of Catholic Church-State relations, it was necessary to use secondary, as well as primary, source materials related to both institutions. In the case of the Catholic Church, all Papal references were taken from the Acta Apostolica Sedis and the Enchiridion Symbolorum, both of which are recognized by Catholic scholars as the official sources of Catholic doctrine. All were taken from the original Latin except for the encyclicals of Pope Leo XIII, which were written before the publication of the first volume of the Acta Apostolica Sedis in 1909. An English compendium, approved by the American Catholic hierarchy was used in the case of the Leonine writings. The documents of Vatican II were also taken from an approved English source. Since statements made at the General Council were translated almost immediately from Latin into English and other foreign languages by periti (experts) and published, the vernacular was used.

All government sources were taken from committee prints, hearings, reports, and other official U.S. government publications. The Congressional Record, the Department of State Bulletin and the Weekly Compilation of Presidential Documents were especially valuable.

The use of primary source materials enabled the author to uncover the work of the American Catholic Church on behalf of international human rights. Much data was obtained from the files of the United States Catholic Conference (USCC), specifically its Office of International Justice and Peace (OIJP), and the National Council of Churches (NCC), its human rights division. Both offices allowed the author complete freedom to read and use their files, as well as to quote from previously unpublished letters, memos, and minutes of inter-agency meetings.

Interviews were also utilized to gain original information. They were conducted with the following individuals and are recorded on tape: Mr. Thomas Quigley, Ms. Patricia Rengel and Father J. Bryan Hehir of the Office of International Justice and Peace of the United States Catholic Conference; Mr. Michael Bennett of the Office of Government Liaison of the United States Catholic Conference, Reverend William Wipfler of the human rights division of the National Council of Churches, Dr. John Salzberg of the Office of Human Rights and Humanitarian Affairs of the

State Department,* and Ms. Alba Zizzamia of the Office of World Justice and Peace of the Diocese of New York.

Other interviews were conducted but not recorded either because it was requested by the individuals being questioned or because it seemed inappropriate at the time. Among those interviewed, but not recorded, were Bishop Peter Gerety of Newark, Congressman Thomas Harkin of Iowa, Father Louis Colonnese, past director of the Latin American Division of the United States Catholic Conference, and Mr. George Lister of the State Department. All the researcher's notes, however, are available to scholars interested in the matter of the Church and human rights.

Correspondence was also used to gather primary source information. Letters from Mr. Thomas Quigley, Ms. Holly Burkthaler, Administrative Assistant to Congressman Harkin, Mayor Donald Fraser of Minneapolis, and Father Louis Colonnese, are also in the author's possession.

Finally, oral histories were taken from persons who participated in early Catholic attempts to work for war relief and human rights. The information provided by Bishop Edward Swanstrom of Catholic Charities of the Diocese of New York, and

---

*The tape made at the State Department is difficult to hear, as some sort of a jamming device was obviously in place.

Ms. Catherine Schaefer now retired and living in Washington, D.C. filled many gaps in the author's data that could not be found elsewhere. This information is also located in the author's notes.

Chapter II: The Beginnings of Catholic Involvement in the Formulation of U.S. Human Rights Policy, 1945-1949.

American Catholic Church-State relations can be characterized as antagonistic well into the twentieth century. This chapter will focus on how those strained relations impacted on early attempts by the Church to play some sort of a role in the formulation of U.S. human rights foreign policy after World War II.

Prior to the 1940's the American Catholic Church had no political clout in the United States. Three situations contributed to that condition. First, the Church adhered to a religious position which demanded that the state protect its freedom and favor its position in society as the divine institution founded by Christ. Reemphasized by Leo XIII in modern times, this stance clearly clashed with the constitutional principle of separation of Church and State.[1] Second, Catholics consciously separated themselves from the rest of American society during the first one hundred and fifty years of U.S. development. Their loyalty to the Pope, immigrant ghettos, religiously segregated schools and distrust of non-Catholics, made them a minority with a mystique, and a growing force to be feared.

1
  Jo Renee Formicola, "American Catholic Political Theory," The Journal of Church and State , XXIX (Autumn 1987): 457-474.

Third, the Church often collided with its religious rivals, the Protestants, over economic, social, education and political matters. Placing the government in the position of arbiter, the Catholic Church and the State were often in conflict over the resolution of such challenges.

World War I, however, gave Catholics a chance to prove their patriotism and dispell the commonly held negative perceptions of their loyalty to America. Although they served with distinction overseas, domestic conditions still conspired to keep them from getting a piece of the American political pie. Their soaring birth rate, increased immigration, growing private schools, and continued Papal loyalty, brought social rejection and a resuscitated nativism in the 1920's. The Catholic quest for political legitimacy was crushed definitively when, one of their own, Al Smith, ended up in an abortive Presidential bid in 1928. Even FDR's attempts to pull Catholics into the political arena in the 1930's had no impact on bringing Catholics into the political mainstream as American became involved in World War II.

The Second World War gave Catholics another chance to prove themselves. The twenty-five intervening years between the start of World War I and the end of World War II brought many societal changes in America, and now, several factors came together which resulted in the embryonic acceptance of Catholics in America. By the 1940's and 1950's, second and third generation Catholics were better educated, economically independent and politically aware.

Progressive theological concepts of Church and State began to reconcile religious/political differences at home. Protestant-Catholic squabbles continued sporadically, but their intensity had, for the most part, waned by the diversion of the War.

In the immediate post-War period, the energies of the American Catholic Church focused on the problem of war relief. And, ironically, the acute need for Church help in this concrete, humanitarian matter helped to forge a better relationship between the American Catholic Church and the United States government.

By the end of World War II, the Truman Administration had already committed itself to participate in programs of War relief. Broadly speaking, these humanitarian efforts were carried out in two ways, multilaterally, through international agreements and associations designed to meet the needs of the victims of the War; and bilaterally, through U.S. agencies also established, at the outset, to aid refugees, but later broadened to work for the regeneration of the devastated areas of the War, as well.

In the multilateral channel, the U.S. government had joined with forty-four other nations during the War* to establish the United Nations Relief and Rehabilitation Administration (UNRRA).

---

*November 9, 1943

Headed by Herbert Lehman, former Governor of New York, the purpose of that international agency was to dispense funds for the humanitarian needs and reconstruction requirements of the nations at war. In 1948, UNRRA was replaced by the International Relief Organization (IRO), an agency of the newly founded United Nations, in which the U.S. participated by assisting in the resettlement and care of displaced persons.

The United States also agreed, at the Breton Woods Conference in 1944, to join with forty-four nations to set up the International Bank for Reconstruction and Redevelopment (IBRD) and to establish the International Monetary Fund (IMF). Both were designed to lend money to the War devastated countries for rebuilding efforts.

The U.S. Government contributions to these international organizations is staggering by any measurement.* However, these efforts were further supplemented by bilateral assistance as well beginning with Lend-Lease in 1941. By 1945, Congress voted to increase and expand the operations of the Export-Import Bank (previously founded in 1934) and set up Government Assistance and Relief in Occupied Areas (GARIOA) to be administered by the army. More significantly, it also authorized a 3.7 billion dollar loan for relief and reconstruction to Great Britain on long-term, negligible interest conditions, thus establishing a precedent for greater involvement in post-War rebuilding assistance. Finally,

---

*For a breakdown of U.S. foreign aid figures from 1943 to 1949 see <u>Congress</u> <u>and</u> <u>the</u> <u>Nation,</u> <u>1945-1964,</u> (Washington: Congressional Quarterly Service, 1965) pp. 163-167.

in 1947, the European Recovery Program (ERP), better known as the
Marshall Plan, was begun. A long range commitment by the U.S. to
complete the task of rebuilding Europe, it was also a commitment
by the sixteen potential European recipients of American foreign
aid to self help and economic reform under American guidance.
Thus by fiscal 1948, the U.S. aid picture included a 6.5 billion
dollar expenditure, of which 4 billion was dispensed as part of
the ERP, 1.3 billion was used for GARIOA, and the rest was given
in military assistance and contributions to relief programs.[2]

    This situation began to change in 1949.   In order to meet
the challange of the Commintern, and Soviet military might in
Eastern Europe, the U.S. joined with its European allies in the
formulation of a military alliance, the North Atlantic Treaty
Organization   (NATO).   Starting in 1949,   then,   aid   for
rehabilitation   was   augmented significantly with funds   for
military   purposes.   Although Congress still continued   to
appropriate large sums to the ERP, funding to NATO members and
other nations allied against Communism increased by   the
disbursement of money for military aid through the Mutual Defense
Assistance Act.   By 1950, then, of 8.5 billion dollars given in
aid, 5.7 was for the purpose of military assistance, and 2.8 for
relief and reconstruction.[3]   The golden age of American

2
  Ibid., p. 166
3
   Ibid.,p. 167

governmental concern for relief and reconstruction began to fade in the light of Soviet military encroachments. Humanitarian needs slowly began to recede as a priority of governmental aid programs, and military assistance began to replace all other considerations.

During the War, and in the immediate post-War period, the Catholic Church had also become involved in relief and humanitarian work. The Vatican took the lead with Pope Pius XII carrying on "tireless activity,"[4] on behalf of War relief efforts. Indeed, while UNRRA was still organizing in 1944, the resources of the Italian government, among them the Italian Red Cross and the Vatican, were temporarily combined to form the National Agency for the distribution of Relief in Italy. "This collaboration proved so effective that it became the basis subsequently for permanent welfare organization in Italy."[5]

During the War and post-War years, the main international concern of the American Catholic Church emerged as the need to give assistance to the victims of the War. Initially, American Catholic War relief efforts were carried out separately from those of the United States government; however, co-operation was evident throughout the post-War period, and some joint efforts in that regard actually occurred by the end of the decade.

---

[4]
Wartime Correspondence Between President Roosevelt and Pope Pius XIII, (New York: Macmillan, 1947), p.106.
[5]
Ibid

The early years of Catholic involvement in war relief, 1943-1946, were an independent effort due to differences in the purpose and methods of the Church and the U.S. government. While the government was committed to a massive, long-term role in the relief and rehabilitation of the nations at war, the Church was concerned more with the acute, short-term human needs of the people. While the government could operate with vast sums of tax money, sometimes through deficit spending, the Church could only dispense limited, voluntary contributions. While the government had to set up the complicated machinery and bureaucracy to get relief services to the people, the Church could use its world-wide facilities, schools, churches and hospitals, as well as call on its missionaries and other personnel already dedicated to humanitarian and charitable works. In short, the Catholic Church could more quickly and deftly handle the relief needs of the war victims until the government could provide more massive assistance later.

The American Catholic Church had been collecting money for War relief since 1940. In those War years, the Bishops' War Relief and Emergency Fund was established to collect money to be sent to Rome to be dispensed by the Holy See as a neutral agent. Other funds were collected by the Bishops all during the War by their annual Laetare Sunday Appeal. These monies, collected in the Churches, provided limited aid to supply Catholic servicemen with religious articles such as prayer books, rosaries and other goods not provided through government services.

In 1943, however, a cooperative effort for War relief assistance between the government and voluntary organizations was effected by the establishment of the National War Fund (NWF). An extension of the Community Chest or United Fund, the National War Fund was founded at the request of the President's War Relief Control Board to eliminate duplicate appeals for War relief. The National War Fund (NWF) was designed to coordinate all voluntary campaigns for War relief and to administer, as well as distribute, those funds to philanthropic organizations approved by the government. These charitable agencies, in turn, would carry out the actual job of War relief. The President of the NWF, Winthrop W. Aldrich, explained:

> The War Fund has taken the position that
> the American people should not be asked
> to contribute to projects which such
> governmental agencies (UNRRA, Lend-Lease)
> are able and willing to finance...In the
> field of foreign relief the resources of
> the War Fund are devoted to supplementary
> and emergency relief projects which can be
> accomplished outside the field occupied by
> governmental agencies or before such agencies
> can be geared up to handle them.
>   Such functions can best be exercised
> by the more flexible action of the private
> relief agencies, and in view of the limited
> funds which can be placed at their disposal,
> supplementary and emergency services is all
> the private agencies can attempt to render. [6]

6
  Winthrop W. Aldrich, "For Our Own and For Our Allies,"
New York Times Magazine, 15 October 1944, pp.13 and 36.

The National War Fund operated in five main areas: service to the armed forces, their auxiliaries and the merchant marine, aid to War prisoners, relief in occupied countries, assistance to unoccupied areas and aid to refugees. The American Catholic Church carried out its humanitarian and relief efforts through the NWF by an already established organ of the Church--the National Catholic Welfare Council (NCWC). By setting up an office of War Relief Services with two special committees, the Catholic Committee for Refugees and the Committee of Relief and War Agencies, the work of the NCWC could be supported by Catholic world-wide religious groups. CARITAS*, and religious orders, particularly the Jesuits, Maryknollers and the St. Vincent de Paul Society, all of whom had previously been involved in humanitarian work in schools and missions around the globe, became involved.

In 1943, Monsignor (later Bishop) Howard Carroll, who was then executive Secretary of the NCWC-War Relief Services, prevailed upon Monsignor (later Bishop) Brian McEntagert, the Director of Catholic Charities in New York, to work with American Catholic businessmen to draw up a "memorandum of understanding" for cooperation with the National War Fund. As a result of Monsignor McEntagert's work, the NCWC-War Relief Services was certified by the NWF as a voluntary international relief agency and granted 1.7 million dollars in that year to carry on

---

*The name given to Catholic Charities abroad.

humanitarian work in No. Africa, Spain, and Portugal. It was also to help with prisoners of war, refugees and seamen.

The next year, 1944, Monsignor (later Cardinal) Patrick O'Boyle, succeeded Monsignor Howard Carroll as director of NCWC-War Relief Services. His assistant, a Father (later Bishop) Edward Swanstrom who had been serving as director of children's services for the Diocese of Brooklyn, eventually replaced Monsignor O'Boyle* as director of NCWC-War Relief Services. Present and in charge almost from its inception to its dismantling after the War, Bishop Swanstrom became an important source of oral history for this study. In an interview in 1980 he discussed the efforts and workings of the Catholic Church on behalf of war relief efforts during and after World War II.

Bishop Swanstrom explained that each year, NCWC-War Relief Services, as well as the other participating voluntary agencies in the NWF, had to present and justify a budget for War relief services to that government body. Fortunately, he reported, due to the work performed by NCWC-War Relief Services, each year its grants became larger, until by 1946, its allocation was the largest received by any voluntary agency, 4.7 million dollars.** The NCWC-War Relief Services organization, having secured funds, would then contact the Catholic Bishops in those countries in

---

7
Interview with Bishop Edward Swanstrom, retired executive director of War Relief Services, May 20, 1980.

*O'Boyle became director of Catholic Charities for the Archdiocese of New York.

**The total received was $12,140,132.00. Figures obtained from Bishop Swanstrom.

need of aid. Their permission would be sought to use Catholic facilities, such as schools, churches, hospitals and missions, as well as personnel, members of religious orders and volunteers, to assist in the delivery of War relief funds and goods. The NCWC-War Relief Services would then approach the government in charge and work out agreements to allow for duty free imports, inland transportation, and warehouse facilities.

In the early days of NCWC-War Relief Services (1943 and 1944), that organization worked primarily in the allied territories, and later its efforts were extended into allied occupied areas. As the war ended, NCWC-War Relief Services played an important role in securing and distributing relief assistance to Germany and its allies, in short, to all countries ravaged by the War.

In 1943 and 1944, the American Catholic Church also cooperated with the War relief efforts of the UNRRA. In 1943, Herbert Lehman, ex-governor of New York and Director General of the UNRRA, admitted that the national government could not do all the work of relief alone, but that the resources of other public and private organizations would also be needed.[8] Bishop Swanstrom felt that although the UNRRA "organized rapidly" and "did a good job", the Catholic Church actually "carried the ball"

8
"Jewish Aid Group to Seek Sixteen Million Dollars," New York Times, 6 December 1943, p. 17.

on early emergency relief, especially through the St. Vincent de Paul Society, world-wide, until the UNRRA could get its machinery and bureaucracy in place.

The Bishop emphasized that "no money ever received from the NWF or UNRRA was ever used for directly religious purposes," and that "all monies and goods were distributed without regard to race, or creed; that the only criterion was need.

In 1946, when the NWF was dismantled, and the government took over most of the War relief work, the American Catholic Church was still so committed to its charitable, international work, that it decided to continue with its War relief efforts. In 1947, the 150 welfare centers of the Catholic Church already established began to be funded entirely from the Bishop's Emergency War Relief Fund. This was a completely private, voluntary solicitation, which raised 7.5 million dollars in the first year of its appeal. Subsequent years brought that total to $11,486,812.37.* This total which has been unpublished until now, reflects the genuine commitment of the Catholic hierarchy and its membership toward War relief, its main international concern, in the post-War years.

It was during this period that Government co-operation with the Church on behalf of its charitable work began to occur. While the Church was providing relief services on its own, Bishop Swanstrom emphasized that the Government provided ships and free

---

*Interview Bishop Swanstrom, May 20, 1980

portage for all relief goods. The lack of a need to pay for shipping, according to Bishop Swanstrom, made the Catholic contribution to the War relief effort even more significant. He revealed, for the first time, that the value of goods collected and distributed by NCWC-War Relief Services amounted to $129,147,385,000, * another indicator of the main Catholic international concern during the War and post-War years. At the same time, the Bishop mentioned that the government donated "substantial amounts" of food which was subsequently distributed by the Church in areas still in need of relief.

When questioned about Church-State relations during the War, Bishop Swanstrom stressed the positive bonds between the American Catholic Church and the U.S. Government on matters of War relief. He claimed that as far as humanitarian matters were concerned, the American Catholic Church-State relationship could be characterized as "good", and that "there was no question about working with Catholic organizations." Further, in spite of the Protestant uproar about the appointment of Myron Taylor as the President's representative to the Vatican, Bishop Swanstrom had nothing but praise for Mr. Taylor's efforts on behalf of War relief. In fact, the Bishop said that his help was most important in expediting and co-ordinating the entire War relief

---

* Interview Bishop Swanstrom, May 20, 1980.

effort.*   And, Bishop Swanstrom, in assessing the role of both
Protestant and Catholic groups in the area of war relief, claimed
that their work was both "ecumenical" and "on a par."

A look back on the post-War years, reveals that the main
American Catholic international concern was how to practically
and physically help the victims of the War.   This Church concern
was manifested and carried out primarily through its charitable
work in all the war torn areas of the world.   American Catholic
concern for the victims of the War was not channelled through
political organs for the purpose of securing theoretical human
rights for those same people.   Rather, the Church concentrated
the bulk of its endeavors in the practical, not the abstract
sphere; in the charitable, not the political, arena after the
War.

II.   The Early Role of the Government and the Church
      in International Human Rights Policy Development

After the War, the U.S. Government became acutely concerned,
not only with the physical needs of the War victims, but with
their civil and political freedoms as well. The U.S. Government,
after all, had been founded on the belief in each individual's

---

*Interestingly this is the role that F.D.R. had envisioned for
Taylor when he appointed him.   He wrote to Pope Pius XII on
December 23, 1939:   "I am therefore suggesting to Your Holiness
that it would give me great satisfaction to send to you my
personal representative in order that our parallel endeavors for
peace and the alleviation of suffering may be assisted."
Wartime Correspondence of Pope Pius XII, op.cit.,p. 4.

right to life, liberty, and the pursuit of happiness. Through the years, as a result of legislation, practice, and Court decisions, it had enlarged and redefined American under-standing of human liberties. By and large,however, the rights protected by the American Constitution were traditionally those rights individuals possessed as citizens or residents of the United States. There was no significant commitment to the protection of international human rights by the government prior to World War II.

In the 19th century, the U.S. government had attempted to deal with the question of the "humane" treatment of combatants and prisoners of war by participating in the Brussels Convention and the Hague Conventions. But these international meetings, in reality, were merely a means to redefine the rules of war, not an attempt to develop some international precepts for the advancement of the basic human rights of all individuals.

At the end of World War I, President Woodrow Wilson, who had attempted to give American's entrance into that war a moral dimension by making the world safe for democracy, tried to establish a sense of international accountability for the actions of states, and a semblance of universal rights, within the framework of the League of Nations. Articles 22 and 23 of that Covenant established responsibilities for which member states would be held liable. Article 22 established the Mandate System, a situation by which one state would administer the affairs of another. It declared:

> ...The Mandatory must be responsible for the administration of the territory under conditions which will guarantee freedom of conscience and religion, subject only to the maintenance of public order and morals, the prohibition of abuses such as the slave trade, the arms traffic and liquor traffic...and will also secure equal opportunities for the free trade and commerce of other Members of the League. 9

Further, Article 22, Section 7 required that the Mandatory Power deliver an annual report of its activities to a Commission set up under Article 22 Section 9. Meanwhile, Article 23 called for the League members to endeavor to secure and maintain fair and humane conditions of labor for men, women and children; and to prohibit the traffic of women, children and drugs. Finally, it called for the limitation of the arms trade, freedom of communications and for positive action against disease. Such international human rights concerns and accountability, however, were rejected as a policy of the United States, by the Congressional decision not to approve the League of Nations Treaty.

Between World War I and World War II, one meeting held at Geneva, Switzerland shored up the principles which were laid down at the Hague Convention of 1907. Possibly due to the violations which occurred during World War I, changes in the world

---

9
Francis P. Walters, A History of the League of Nations (New York: Oxford University Press, 1952), pp. 57ff. This is Section 5 of Article 22.

configurations of power and technology, as well as a floundering system of international law, the community of nations again felt it necessary to discuss the rules of war. At that meeting, three conventions were passed: the Red Cross Convention, the Convention on the Treatment of Prisoners of War, and the Convention for the Amelioration of the Condition of the Wounded and Sick in the Armies in the Field. Essentially, however, these agreements again dealt with the treatment of combatants and did not set down any precedents for the protection of the human rights of non-beligerents.

Only one significant treaty was entered into by the United States Government between 1789 and 1945 on a matter of human rights other than humane war behavior. In 1926, the International Convention to Suppress Slave Trade and Slavery was signed. An extension of the General Act of the Brussels Conference (1889-1890), it gave support to the Convention of St. Germain-en-Laye in 1919, neither of which were able to resolve the matter of slave trade up to that time. It was also the culmination of efforts by the United States and Great Britain in the Treaty of Ghent (1814)* and the Webster-Ashburton Treaty

---

*The primary purpose of the meeting at Ghent was to end the War of 1812 and to settle the matter of blockades and the impressment of American sailors. Slavery was but a side issue.

(1842) * to abolish the business of slavery.**

Thus, on the eve of World War II, the United States Government had committed itself to protect the civil and political rights of its citizens and residents, to participate humanely in war, and to work for the suppression of the international slave trade. But, its international human rights commitment could be characterized as negligible.

With the outbreak of war, however, F.D.R. went before the Congress and redefined the Four Freedoms on which America was founded: freedom from want, freedom from fear, freedom of expression and freedom of religion. Incorporated into the Atlantic Charter in 1941, these principles became the ideological basis for the American support of the Allies and the philosophical justification for U.S. entrance into World War II.

In 1941, the President communicated his feelings about international human rights to Pope Pius XII at Easter time:

---

*The main purpose of the Webster-Asburton Treaty was to settle the boundary between Maine and Canada. Again, slavery was an insignificant matter.

**The convention to Suppress Slave Trade and Slavery was augmented by a similar treaty in the United Nations in 1956, which called for intensified efforts to abolish slavery. Finally, the United States acceded and ratified these conventions completely in 1957.

... So long as the human spirit is undefeated,
the great elementary human freedoms will in-
evitably be triumphant. Here in the United
States we believe that freedom of worship is
the first and greatest need of us all. For
that reason we have exerted all our influence
against religious persecutions, which for
the first time in centuries again threaten
the brotherhood of man in many parts of the
world. We have likewise sought freedom of
information so that no conqueror can enslave
men's minds or prevent them from finding their
way to the truth. We have set our minds to
attaining freedom from fear, so that no man,
no family, no nation, need live perpetually
under the shadow of danger from bombs, invasion,
and ensuing devastation. And we propose to
forward the cause of freedom from want by direct
relief where this is possible and necessary and
by so improving the economic processes of life
that children may be born and families may be
reared in safety and comfort. 10

Pope Pius answered the President with similar sentiments.

We have not failed and We shall not fail to
do everything possible to alleviate the suf-
ferings of those in need, and in carrying out
this beneficent work of charity. We have found
unbounded sympathy and generous co-operation
among Our beloved children in the United States.
Not content with this, We have felt, and We feel
it Our duty, to raise our voice, the voice of a
Father not moved by any earthly interest, but
animated only by a desire for the common good
of all, in a plea for a peace that will be
genuine, just, honorable and lasting, a peace
that will respect individuals, families, and
nations and safeguard their rights to life,
to a reasonable liberty, to a conscientious
and fervent practice of religion, to true
progress, and to an equitable participation
in the riches which providence has distributed
with a largess over the earth...11

10
   Wartime Correspondence of Pope Pius XII,op.cit.,p.51
11
   Ibid., p.53.

Both the President of the United States and the Pope of the Catholic Church evidenced an early concern, not only for the physical well-being of the War victims (freedom from want), but for their spiritual well-being also (freedom from fear). This concern became an acute preoccupation of the U.S. government, causing it to secure the protection of international civil, political, social and religious rights for others after the War. Channelling its efforts to accomplish this primarily through international bodies, the government seized the opportunity to work through the newly proposed United Nations. On the other hand, the American Catholic Church, also concerned with these same problems, was still so totally committed to the War relief effort that it took little political action to advance international human rights. Consequently, the Church found itself playing only a peripheral role in the formulation of U.S. human rights foreign policy due to its own lack of interest and because the U.S. government sought to develop such a policy on the recommendations of international organizations rather than on those of specific, domestic interest groups.

Demonstrating its commitment to international human rights immediately after the War, the American government participated in the Four Power Agreement on Crimes Against Humanity. As the victorious Allies drafted the Charter of the International Military Tribunal, specifically to prosecute those Nazis guilty of crimes against humanity, it became necessary to first reach a consensus and define some of the international rights of all individuals.

Article Six of the Charter clearly outlined war crimes. They included 1) the murder, ill-treatment, or deportation of civilians to slave labor, 2) the murder or ill-treatment of prisoners of war, or persons on the seas, 3) the killing of hostages, 4) the plunder of public private property and 5) the unnecessary destruction of towns and cities. More importantly, that document enumerated crimes against humanity, and set a standard of basic rights to be respected for all time. The crimes against humanity included murder, extermination, enslavement, deportations and persecution for political or racial reasons. Unfortunately, these principles only served as the basis to prosecute and convict particular Nazi war criminals at Nuremburg and did not extend beyond the scope of crimes committed during World War II.

During the post-War years, 1945-1949, the American Catholic Church was concerned with international human rights in a minor way, its prime interest being War relief. Although the Christmas messages of Pope Pius XII in 1942 and 1944 called for universal support of personal and civil rights, the American Catholic Church did not pursue such goals with the same intensity as it promoted its charitable, international work during those same years. Nevertheless, the American Catholic hierarchy, through the National Catholic Welfare Council (NCWC), an American Catholic lay group, the Catholic Association for International Peace (CAIP), and two international Catholic Women's Groups, the World Union of Catholic Women's Organizations and the Catholic

International Union for Social Service, worked to discuss and draft an international bill of rights. The Catholic Church also made policy statements on human rights, participated at the San Francisco Conference for the establishment of the United Nations and was involved in the drafting of the U.N. Universal Declaration of Human Rights in 1948.

The early contributions of American Catholic organizations to the development of a potential human rights policy were negligible: a 1941 attempt by CAIP to draft an international bill of rights, a joint statement with Protestants and Jews in 1943 on a "Pattern for Peace", and another declaration with them in 1945 on "Goals for San Francisco".[12] However, with a government invitation to both the NCWC and the CAIP to attend the San Francisco Conference on the United Nations in 1946 as Non-government organizations (NGOs) with consultant status, the Catholic Church had an opportunity to play a limited role, at least, in helping to establish U.S. human rights priorities. Of forty-eight NGOs invited to the San Francisco Conference, only two were Catholic. The delegates to the conference were Mr. Richard Pattee and Mr. James F. Grady for the NCWC; and Mr. Thomas F. Mahoney and Ms. Catherine Schaefer for the CAIP. The records of the NGO meetings are the property of the United Nations, uncatalogued, and not available to the public.

_____

12
For a discussion of these early policy statements see: Wilfred Parsons, S.J., "Declaration of Human Rights. A Major Hope of Afflicted Humanity", Catholic Mind, March 1948, pp. 146-156.

Fortunately, Ms. Schaefer, who was then the Assistant Executive Director of CAIP* gave two interviews to the author in 1980, and revealed information that has not been previously published about the Catholic participation at the San Francisco Conference to establish the U.N., and the Lake Success meetings to draft the Universal Declaration of Human Rights. She sketched out the following role of the Catholics and the other NGOs at the San Francisco Conference.

When the U.N. forming-body met, its aim was essentially to create a world organization to promote peace and security. However, the American delegation, along with Panama and other Latin American nations, were prodded by the non-governmenal organizations to include a Bill of Rights as part of the Covenant of the United States. Schaefer pointed out that all the NGOs had daily access to Mr. Harold Stassen, the American representative of the United States delegation. They could discuss and make suggestions to him at that time. She claimed that it was the combined recommendations of the NGOs that a special commission be set up to discuss human rights after the Convention was ended. As a result of this suggestion, this actually occurred later, when the American delegation pressed for such a follow-up. The matter of drafting a specific human rights proposal was taken up

*The Executive Director of CAIP was Father Raymond McGowan, who had been assistant to Father John A. Ryan at the Social Department of NCWC earlier. Ms. Schaefer's information and opinions are not footnoted each time a quotation appears, but each quote is attributed to conversations held on May 8,1980 and June 11, 1980.

at Lake Success, New York in 1947. Other writers pointed out that:

> All of this copious recognition by the U.N.
> Charter of 'human rights and fundamental
> freedoms' came about as a result of a long
> and arduous campaign conducted mostly by the
> religious forces of the nations, ably seconded
> by Latin American statesmen and a few others. 13

In an article by Schaefer, she pointed out that:

> Due largely to the efforts of U.S. non-governmental
> organizations, including the NCWC and the CAIP, the
> NCWC and the CAIP, the international recognition of
> the importance of human rights began simultaneously
> with the formal recognition of the physical unity
> of the world organization in the establishement of
> the United Nations. 14

In 1946, the United Nations General Assembly passed a resolution calling for the creation of a Commission on Human Rights, and directed that it was to meet in January of 1947, for the first time. Schaefer was present again at these discussions held at Lake Success, having been sent by NCWC to set up an office for U.N. affairs, to supply NCWC with information on the meeting, and to inform the delegates of the Catholic stand on human rights. At that time (1947) she was not an invited participant and had no official status there. In fact, no strictly American organizations were asked to attend; all invited agencies had to apply first and then show international status and involvement.

13
  Ibid., p. 143.

14
  Catherine Schaefer, "We the Peoples and Human Rights",
Catholic Action, May 1949, p. 4.

Two international Catholic organizations, however, did apply and were granted consultant status at the Commission's meetings: The World Union of Catholic Women's Organizations, based in Geneva and formerly active in League of Nations humanitariam endeavors; and the Catholic International Union for Social Service, located in Belgium and committed to social justice. Because Schaefer was already physically present, and because she had also worked actively for human rights in San Francisco, the World Union of Catholic Women's Organizations asked her to serve as their representative. Dr. Alice Vergara and Mrs. Grace Aieta acted as the delegates for the Catholic International Union for Social Services.

To draw up an international bill of rights was the task of the Commission on Human Rights. Although the Charter of the U.N. called for the protection of human rights in Article 55, no specifics had been mentioned previously.

The challange was momentus: to try to reconcile many different value systems and philosophies. Essentially three views of rights had to be synthesized: the Soviet view, which stressed the responsibility of man to the state; the French view, which emphasized social responsiblities; and the consensus of the Commission, which supported the belief in natural rights. Bringing these divergent views together fell to Mrs. Eleanor Roosevelt, the American representative, who was elected the Commission's head. Schaefer recalled that although the consultants had access to Mrs. Roosevelt, and although she tried to be fair and impartial, a definite "reserve" could be felt in her attitude toward the Cathoilcs. Nevertheless, in three regular sessions and in two drafting meetings, the Commission produced the now famous Universal Declaration of Human Rights within a year.

Schaefer wrote that:

> ...not only the government delegates but the...non-governmental organizations contributed to the careful and arduous writing of this Declaration. Because it dealt with the essential nature of man, child of God, the Catholics of the world were in the forefront with recommendations for its proper formulation. 15

Schaefer's allusion to "recommendations", in reality, was to the Declaration of Rights published in February 1947 by a committee appointed by the NCWC for presentation to the Committee on Human Rights. In that document, the American Bishops officially stated their views on the rights of the individual, the family, the State and the community of nations. The document bears study, not only because it was the first significant American Catholic statement on international human rights, but because it still serves as a model of Catholic concern for universal human rights today.

15
   Ibid., p. 5.

The preamble of the Declaration of Rights [16] reaffirmed basic Catholic beliefs: that man is created by God, with obligations to his Creator, himself, his neighbor, the state and the world. To be denied the opportunity to discharge such reponsibilities would violate man's natural, unalienable rights which are the basis of the moral law known by reason.

Part I of the Declaration of Rights discussed the rights of the human person. These included the right of life and bodily integrity "from the moment of conception" [17] the right to serve and worship God in private and in public, and the right to religious freedom. Also mentioned were the right to liberty, equal protection under the law, the right to freedom of expression, the right to choose one's state in life, the right to an education, and the right to petition the government. Further, it supported the right of every individual to have a nationality, to work and migrate, to associate and assemble. Not excluded were the right to choose one's occupation, to private ownership, to a living wage, to bargain collectively, to join in work associations and to receive assistance from society when in distress.

The concept of the rights of the family were a significantly Catholic contribution to the development of human rights, as shall be seen later. In Part II, the Declaration called for the right of all persons to marry and have children, as well as to

---

16
National Cathoic Welfare Conference, "Declaration of Rights", reprinted in Catholic Mind, April 1947, pp. 193-6.
17
Ibid., p. 194.

obtain economic security for the maintenance of the family. It supported the right to the protection of maternity, the right to educate one's children, the right to maintain adequate child welfare, public child care assistance, immunity from house search and trespass, and the right to be protected against immoral conditions within the society.

In Part III, the rights of the states were enumerated. Encompassing the right to enact just laws, to establish courts and enforce the law, that section also stressed respect for minorities, the right to tax, the right of eminent domain, the right to demand an educated citizenry, the right to defend itself, the right to restrain groups for the common good, and the right to act in emergencies to protect the common good.

The rights of the State in the international community were listed in Part IV and were founded on the premise that there was a need for peaceful relations based on respect. Defending the right of the state to exist, to self determination, to juridicial equality, and membership in the international community, the Declaration of Rights also recognized that these rights entitled all states to secure the help of the community of nations for a redress of grievances. It also included the right to revise treaties, to use international procedures to settle disputes, to have access to world markets, to protect natural resources, to receive aid, and to grant asylum.

The significance of the publication of this document during the first session of the meeting of the Commission on Human Rights, according to Schaefer, was that it "was presented to members of the Commission and it figured prominently in its early discussions and received wide attention in the press.[18] Laying the groundwork for the positions which the Catholic delegates advanced at the Lake Success meetings was also a result of the NCWC Declaration of Rights. Essentially Schaefer said their stance was based on a natural law concept of human rights and on traditional Catholic moral teachings. Among these were attempts to emphasize the Divine source of human life, and to expand the right to life to include a prohibition against abortion. Stressing the right to marriage and the family and trying to eliminate the right to divorce as a tenet of the Universal Declaration of Human Rights was also a goal of the Catholic delegates. They sought to influence other delegates to work for the right of parents to choose the type of education they preferred for their children, and the right of individuals to pick their own vocation, even the religious life. These notions, according to Schaefer, were supported by "many memoranda and articles". Of those Catholic ideas emphasized, however, many were rejected by the full Commission.[19]

18
    Schaefer, op. cit., p. 5.

19
    See Rita Schaefer, "United Nations and Human Rights", Catholic Action, July-August 1948, pp. 6-7.

The Universal Declaration of Human Rights does not make mention of God as the author of life; indeed the word "God" cannot be found in the document. The Declaration, rather, is a political statement, whose purpose it is to establish a common standard of achievement by espousing a composite view of human rights. Abortion is not specifically denied, nor is it sanctioned. Divorce is not rejected or approved, although the term "dissolution" of marriage* is used and accepted in the context of the Universal Declaration of Human Rights.

The agreement to include a section on the rights of family is considered by Catholics to be their most significant contribution to the development of a standard of human rights in the Declaration.[20] Elaborating the rights of the parents to choose the type of education they prefer for their children,** that document also recognizes the family as the fundamental unit of society worthy of protection.***

Even though the Catholic organizations were not able to influence the Commission on Human Rights significantly, Schaefer said that, on the whole, their relationship with the Commission was "very good" and that they also "worked very closely" with Protestant and Jewish groups to support religious freedom.

---

*See Article 16, Paragraph 1.

[20] See "U.N. Declaration of Human Rights", *America*, July 3, 1948, P. 304.

** See Article 26, Paragraph 3.

*** See Article 16, Paragraph 3.

Schaefer also felt that the Universal Declaration of Human Rights was a "testament to the long tradition of Catholic teaching".[21]

Thus, looking back over the post-War years, it is now possible to see why the beginnings of Catholic concern for human rights began. Growing out of its traditional function as helper and servant of mankind, the Church saw as its first responsibility, after the War, the duty to restore economic well-being and hope to the victims of that conflict. Its involvement in the acute, charitable, practical needs of the War far outweighed its concern for the more theoretical aspects of the long-term, social and political needs of the victims of World War II. Although the commitment to the War relief effort did siphon off Catholic interest in international human rights, it also had the side effect of establishing better Catholic-government relations after the War. Thus, a small step was made to improve Catholic credibility in the political arena even though no strong effort was made by the Church in the area of human rights foreign policy development.

Several additional reasons account for the limited role that the Church played in the formulation of post-War human rights foreign policy. In its NGO capacity, the American Catholic Church could function only in a modest advisory role. It lacked prestigious hierarchial leadership and international requirements; and it supported dogmatic rather than broad

---

21
Schaefer interview, op. cit.

principles. The efforts of the U.S. government on behalf of human rights were carried out essentially through international organizations, e.g., the International Military Tribunal and the United Nations, and the only role that could be assigned to NGOs, including the Church, was that of consultant. With no vote and no real status, all NGOs, including the Church, could play only a modest role in influencing the American delegation. At the same time, however, the American Catholic Church did not send any influential members of its hierarchy or intelligensia to attend either the San Francisco U.N. Conference or the Lake Success human rights meetings. The Protestants had sent Walter Van Kirk, President of the Federal Council of Churches,and O. Frederick Nolde, head of the Commission of the Churches on International Affairs, among others. The Jewish organizations had sent as one of their representatives, Dr. Moses Moskowitz, the eminent author of many works on human rights. But no really influential American religious or lay person participated on behalf of the Catholic Church.* The choice of Catholic representatives to San Francisco and Lake Success remains a puzzlement.

International status requirements for organizations participating at Lake Success also effectively eliminated American Catholic involvement at that Conference. Catholic

*The Vatican did send Archbishop Cheli as an observer.

representation fell merely to two international women's groups while the NCWC could only play the passive part of an observer. One must wonder why the Vatican itself, as an international organization, did not participate at the Lake Success meetings to draw up the Universal Declaration of Human Rights. This also remains an unanswered question.

The influence of the Church in the formlulation of U.S. human rights foreign policy after the War was also limited by Catholic efforts to support dogmatic beliefs which were often unacceptable to other religious groups and national delegations. Catholic endeavors to block recommendations in support of abortion and divorce were unpopular, and as a result, Catholic influence on other matters of human rights was necessarily diluted.

Looking at a balance sheet of Catholic contributions to the formlulation of post-War human rights foreign policy development, reveals a page with but a few promising entries. Short of one major hierarchial statement on human rights, work in coalition with other NGO's at San Francisco to call for the inclusion of human rights in the U.N. Charter, and the incorporation of the Catholic views on family and educational rights in the Universal Declaration of Human Rights, Catholic influence on post-War human rights foreign policy was modest, at best.

CHAPTER III: COMPLACENCY AND THE SEEDS OF AMERICAN CATHOLIC
              INTEGRATION, 1950-1965

I. Introduction

This chapter will ask two questions.   First, what was the
U.S. human rights foreign policy during the years 1950-1965, and
what was the attitude of the American Catholic Church toward it?
Second, what factors were at work, during those same years, which
helped to integrate American Catholics into the U.S. social and
political mainstream and create a climate in which the Church
would be able to play a positive role in the formulation of a
U.S. human rights foreign policy in the 1970's?

Beginning in 1954, United States policy toward international
human rights became one of informal encouragement, rather than
one of active support reenforced by treaty obligation.   The
American Catholic Church did nothing to oppose what was, in
effect, a government strategy designed to minimize the importance
of international human rights in foreign policy.

In retrospect, both the Church and the government became
complacent about human rights during the 1950's and 1960's. That
attitude evolved out of a concern for the growing Communist
threat, and a distrust of U.S. human rights policy strongly
influenced by United Nations covenants.   In response, both the
government and the Church redirected their international
interests during the Cold War years.   The government shifted its
emphasis in foreign affairs from a concern for the economic,

social and political betterment of the victims of the War, to a concern for the military defense of the world's anti-Communist nations. At the same time, as the Congress began to question the validity of U.S. human rights policy based on U.N. covenants, the Eisenhower Administration shifted the U.S. commitment to human rights from a legally binding obligation to one of informal support. The Church, also, readjusted its international concerns. In response to the Communist threat, the Catholic Church reasserted its own traditional hostility toward its atheistic, materialistic, enemy and supported government anti-Communist policies at home and abroad. In the matter of human rights, the Church also followed the lead of the U.S. government and, by its silence, approved a policy to limit the legal enforcement of U.N. human rights covenants in the Cold War years.

American Catholic support for government human rights and anti-Communist policies had ironic results. On the one hand, it diluted Catholic concern for international human rights, but on the other hand, it served to integrate Catholics into the American mainstream by making them appear to be truly "American". Indeed, both anti-Communism and Catholicism soon became synonymous and were equated with Americanism.

During the decades of the 1950's and 1960's, several other forces were at work which served to integrate Catholics into the American social and political mainstream. The rapid development of a significant native Catholic population, the lessening of religious prejudice, the "Americanization" of Catholicism, and the attempt of the Church to renew and reform itself through Vatican II, brought about a change in the attitude of both Catholics and Protestants towards each other. Indeed, these decades may be characterized as a time when the integrating forces of American society were able to neutralize past religious antagonisms and create a functional religious pluralism. As a result, the beginning of cooperation between Catholics and Protestants could be felt. Catholics were admitted to the political arena. The Church started to commit itself more to social, rather than institutional, concerns in America. As a result of these serendipitous occurrences during the years 1950-1965, the American Catholic Church gained the time, the experience, and the expertise in the U.S. political arena to ready itself to play a positive role in the formulation of U.S. international human rights foreign policy in the next decade.

II. U.S. Human Rights Foreign Policy in the Cold War Years
A. The Bricker Amendment

The attitude of the United States government toward human rights in the Cold War years can best be described as complacent. In Chapter II, it was shown that significant government concern for the political and civil rights of the victims of World War II was manifested in U.S. support of U.N. human rights covenants in the immediate post-War years. However, as the Soviet Union grew stronger and posed a military threat to Europe and Asia after the

War, the U.S. government reordered its international priorities. By replacing foreign aid for rehabilitation by military assistance to halt the Communist encroachments around the world, human rights received less and less attention. Although most U.S. activity with regard to human rights was carried out through the United Nations into the 1950's, early in the decade, members of the Congress, and certain interest groups, feared that the U.S. involvement with the U.N. would result in the U.S. losing control of its ability to form its own human rights policy in the future. They were also concerned that states would be at the mercy of treaty law and would have to conform to U.N. covenants in the matter of U.S. civil rights. There were also suspicions that the Communists were using U.N. human rights covenants to force unwanted racial changes in the United States.

During the period 1948-1952, the United Nations drafted several significant human rights conventions * to which the

---

* Among these were the Convention on Refugees, the Slavery Convention, the Convention on Racial Discrimination, the Genocide Convention, the Convention on Consent to Marriage and the Supplementary Convention on Slavery. However, the Senate Judiciary Committee estimated that over 200 human rights conventions were passed and involved the United States. See: U.S. Congress, Senate, Constitutional Amendments Relative to Treaties and Executive Agreements. Senate Report 412, 83rd. Cong., 1st Sess., June 15, 1953. Herein referred to as the Bricker Hearings. Other estimates showed that the U.S. was party to only 6 conventions and that only 54 were passed by the U.N. See: Arthur Krock, "Inquiry by Arthur Krock to the State Department", New York Times, 5 February, 1954, p. 18. The point is that, at the time, no one was sure how committed the U.S. government was to an unspecified number of human rights conventions.

United States government became party. At the same time, a strange precedent was occurring. The American courts were being petitioned to consider Articles 55 and 56 of the United Nations Charter, which called broadly for the protection of human rights, as legally binding and applicable in cases where the property rights of Orientals and Blacks were being violated. Although the Universal Declaration of Human Rights, which enumerated the rights mentioned in Articles 55 and 56 of the United Nations Charter, was not considered as a treaty, Articles 55 and 56 had been ratified by the Senate and were thought,by some Congressmen, to have the force of law. Indeed, some Congressmen believed that these articles could supercede both federal and state law. Because the Supreme Court had decided in 1920, in the case of Missouri vs. Holland[1] that treaty law took precedence over any conflicting national laws, it was argued that leglislation on any legal agreements which violated the basic human rights of minorities could be considered unconstitutional. This was essentially the argument made by the plaintiffs in Oyama vs. California,[2] Shelley vs. Kraemer,[3] and Sei Fujii vs. State of California,[4] during the period 1948-1952.

---

[1]
252 U.S. 416 (1920).
[2]
332 U.S. 633-688 (1948).
[3]
334 U.S. 1-23 (1948).
[4]
38 Cal. 2nd 718 (1952).

In both Oyama and Sei Fujii, actions were brought against the State of California to invalidate that state's Alien Land Law which denied foreigners the right to own real property. In Oyama, that law was struck down, and in a concurring opinion, four Supreme Court Justices based their decision, not only on the Fourteenth Amendment, but on Articles 55 and 56 of the United Nations Charter as well. In Sei Fujii, the plaintiff argued that Articles 55 and 56 superceded state law. However, the decision and reasoning in that case were ultimately based on the fact that the Court held the Alien Land Law to be in violation of the Fourteenth Amendment.

In Shelley vs. Kraemer, however, the question was whether or not a court enforced private agreement was valid if that agreement was designed to exclude certain races (black) from ownership or occupancy of real property. An amicus brief was filed by the American Association for the United Nations by Alger Hiss, and others, claiming that Articles 55 and 56 had transformed human rights from a domestic to an international matter. Although the Court did not deal with this particular argument, the brief caught the attention of Senator John Bricker (R-Ohio), who later introduced an amendment to limit the U.S. participation in U.N. human rights covenants. Bricker also used Hiss' involvement in the case to show that U.N. human rights policies were in accord with Communist ideas and could be used to bring about Soviet aims in the United States.[5]

The actions of the United Nations with regard to human rights conventions, and the proliferation of cases using Articles 55 and 56 of the U.N. Charter as bases for minority suits against the States, led opponents of self-executing treaty law, particularly the American Bar Association (ABA), to try to take action to limit the "abuses" of the executive agreement and the erosion of legislative power in the areas of foreign affairs and civil rights. A first attempt was made in 1952, when the ABA prevailed upon Senator Arthur Watkins (R-Utah), to introduce Senate Joint Resolution 43, a bill authored by the ABA. It called for a constitutional amendment to limit the President's authority in foreign affairs by subjecting executive agreements to Senate approval, as was the case in treaties. In effect, Senate Joint Resolution 43 was an attempt to halt the President's use of the Executive Agreement to commit the U.S. to U.N. human rights conventions without Senate consent.

After making little headway, the bill was reintroduced on 7 February 1952, for a second time with different language, but with a similar content, as Senate Joint Resolution 130. Although its author, Senator John Bricker, had the support of 58 Senators

------

5
    John W. Bricker and Charles A. Webb, "The Bricker Amendment: Treaty Law vs. Domestic Constitutional Law", Notre Dame Lawyer 29 (August 1954): p. 539.

his committee was not able to complete its work in time to vote the bill out to the entire Senate by the end of its session in 1952. Postponed until 7 January 1953, the bill was brought up for a third time, again by Senator Bricker, and retitled Senate Joint Resolution 1. By then it had the growing support of 63 Senators.

The proposed constitutional amendment of the American Bar Association and Senator John Bricker generated much controversy during the year. Its six short sections speak for themselves.

> Section 1. A provision of a treaty which denies or abridges any right enumerated in this Constitution shall not be of any force or effect.
> Section 2. No treaty shall authorize or permit any foreign power or any international organization to supervise, control, or adjudicate rights of citizens of the United States within the United States enumerated in this Constitution or any other matter essentially within the domestic jurisdiction of the United States.
> Section 3. A treaty shall become effective as international law in the United States only through the enactment of appropriate legislation by the Congress.
> Section 4. All executive or other agreements between the President and any international organization, foreign power, or official thereof shall be made only in the manner and to the extent to be prescribed by law. Such agreements shall be subject to the limitations imposed on treaties, or the making of treaties, by this article.
> Section 5. The Congress shall have power to enforce this article by appropriate legislation.
> Section 6. This article shall be inoperative unless it shall have been ratified as an amendment to the Constitution by the legislatures of three-fourths of the several States within seven years from the date of its submission. 6

6
Bricker Hearings, op. cit., p. 1

The disputes over the bill revolved around three main Constitutional issues: federal law vs. treaty law, states rights, and congressional regulation of executive agreements.[7] However, it was the underlying issue, the fear of the formulation of international human rights policy made at the U.N., that really focused these Constitutional principles to be tested. Senator Bricker wrote:

> Many opponents of SJR 1... seek to elevate treaty law above domestic constitutional law. They seek to ground the whole spectrum of human rights--civil, political, economic, social and cultural--in a law superior to that of the nation. Obviously, the correlative duties would also be made independent of national law...Stripped of all flowery abstractions, the naked question raised by a universal bill of rights is whether or not nations are willing to subordinate domestic constitutional law to a higher treaty law. [8]

And, finally, the rux of Bricker's argument was revealed:

> Not until novel treaties began to roll off the U.N. assembly lines, however, did the domestic problem of self-executing treaties become acute...In considering such treaties, the Senate does not have, as a practical matter, a free hand in writing reservations ....If the Supreme Court holds Articles 55 and 56 as obligatory and self-executing, thousands of federal and state laws will be nullified....[9]

---

[7]
For a debate on the Constitutional issues see Bricker and Webb, op.cit., and Brunson Mac Chesney, "Fallacies in the Case for the Bricker Amendment", Notre Dame Lawyer 29 (August 1954): 551-82.

[8]
Bricker and Webb, op.cit., pp. 533 and 535.

[9]
Ibid, pp. 537 and 539.

Bricker's attacks on the United Nations rights covenants gained momentum as SJR 1 was set for hearings. These lasted from February until April of 1953 and drew witnesses from academia, law, labor, government, religion and numerous other lobby groups. Conspicuously absent from the roster of those testifying, however, was a representative of the Catholic Church.[10]

B. The Eisenhower Compromise

The most significant witness to appear before the Bricker Committee was the Secretary of State, John Foster Dulles. He had come from the Eisenhower Administration to allay the fears of those who believed that national sovereignty, states rights and legislative power would be severely compromised by the continued use of the executive agreement to legally bind the U.S. to self-executing U.N. human rights covenants. Without conceding any executive authority, Dulles tried to minimize the Congressional fears of U.N. self-executing treaties and the Presidential use of the Executive Agreement. He testified that "the treaty making power is not an unlimited power",[11] that "treaties...only rank on an equality with congressional enactments",[12] that "any treaty as international law can be overcome by a simple act of Congress".[13]

10
The Methodists were represented by their witness, Charles F. Boss, the American Jewish Congress by Will Maslow, The National Tabernacle by Rev. De Loss M. Scott and the Christian Scientists by James Watt.
11
Bricker Hearings, op.cit., p. 824.
12
Ibid.
13
Ibid.

He soothed the Senators by saying "This administration is committed to the exercise of the treaty making power only within traditional limits", while admitting that "I do not believe that treaties should or lawfully can be used as a device to circumvent the constitutional procedures established in relation to what are essentially matters of domestic concern".[14]

Obviously, concessions had to be made by the Eisenhower Administration to save the right of the President to make executive agreements and stave off the passage of the Bricker Amendment. Dulles had to promise that the Eisenhower Administration would no longer sign, or become party to U.N. human rights covenants. This capitulation resulted in the end of formal U.S. support for international human rights. Instead, U.S. government policy shifted radically.

> 1. The present administration intends to encourage the promotion everywhere of human rights and individual freedoms, but to favor methods of persuasion, education, and example rather than formal undertakings which commit one part of the world to impose its particular social and moral standards upon another part of the world community, which had different standards...
> Therefore, while we shall not withhold our counsel from those who seek to draft a treaty or covenant on human rights, we do not ourselves look upon a treaty as the means which we would now select as the proper and most effective way to spread throughout the world the goals of human liberty to which this Nation has been dedicated since its inception. We therefore do not intend to become a party to any such covenant or present it as a treaty for consideration by the Senate.

14
Ibid., p. 825.

2. This administration does not intend to sign the Convention on Political Rights of Women. This is not because we do not believe in the equal political status of men and women, or because we shall not seek to promote that equality. Rather it is because we do not believe that this goal can be achieved by treaty coercion or that it constitutes a proper field for exercise of the treaty-making power. We do not now see any clear or necessary relation between the interest and welfare of the United States and the eligibility of women to political office in other nations.

These same principles will guide our action in other fields which have been suggested by some as fields for multilateral treaties.

3. The Constitution provides that the President shall have power to make treaties by and with the advice and consent of the Senate. This administration recognizes the significance of the word "advice". It will be our effort to see that the Senate gets its opportunity to advise and consent in time so that it does not have to choose between adopting treaties it does not like, or embarrassing our international position by rejecting what has already been negotiated out with foreign governments. 15

In essence, then, Dulles conceded that the Eisenhower Administration would promote international human rights only informally. He assured the Congress that the United States would not sign U.N. human rights conventions with the intention of sending them to the Senate, nor would it recognize those covenants as treaties binding on the United States. Realistically, Dulles made a "gentlemen's agreement" with the Congress promising its members that the U.S. would not pursue any policies which might impose obligations on the federal or state governments with regard to civil rights. These executive assurances served to sway enough states rightists who feared that

---

15
  Ibid.

the United Nations would play a role in resolving developing U.S. racial problems. In a close vote on 17 February 1954, the Bricker Amendment was barely defeated 43-44 in favor of a compromise which was also killed later.

The strategy outlined by Dulles to support international human rights without benefit of treaty status became the basic human rights policy of the United States until 1975. In fact, within that twenty year period, only the Convention on Refugees and the Slavery Convention were signed by America's U.N. Ambassador, and ratified by the Senate. The Convention on Racial Discrimination and the Genocide Convention were signed at the U.N. but not ratified by the Senate. Of the other eight human rights conventions, including the Convention on Economic, Social and Cultural Rights and the Convention on Civil and Political Rights, none were signed by the U.S. Ambassador at the U.N. or acted upon by the U.S. Congress before 1975.[16] Thus, the Eisenhower compromise held in abeyance any significant government initiatives or formal support for United Naitons international human rights endeavors for two decades.

C. Catholic Attitude Toward Human Rights

During the Cold War years, the American Catholic Church

---

[16] U.S. Congress, House, *International Protection of Human Rights*, 93rd. Cong., 1st sess., 1973, pp. 797-802. See Appendix 29, "Status of Multilateral Treaties in the Field of Human Rights, Concluded Under the Auspices of the United Nations: The Memorandum of the Secretary General".

did little to support a strong U.S. international human rights policy. Like the government, the Church had become complacent about such concerns in the two decades after the War. Occupied with its own domestic interests, how to obtain power equal to its growing population and how to become integrated into the American mainstream, the American Catholic Church took no official, political or public hierarchial stand to oppose the Bricker Amendment. Only a few Catholic periodicals voiced displeasure with the Congressional challenge to the post-war U.S. human rights policy. Generally, however, the Catholic Church was involved only peripherally in the constitutional, yet moral, dilemma posed by the Bricker Amendment.

A review of the Catholic literature during the Bricker controversy attests to the lack of American Catholic concern for the human rights problems at that time, as only a few sparse articles were uncovered on the subject. Even America and Commonweal, the most widely circulated Catholic magazines of the time had but a few comments regarding the Bricker Amendment. Those were commentaries on the power struggle between the executive and the legislature, rather than on the decline of United States international human rights policy. Wilfred Parsons wrote in America: "It is one of those matters of simple yes or no: our present Constitution or a new one".[17] Other writers in

---

[17] Wilfred Parsons, "Washington Front: The Bricker Reform", America, February 13, 1954, p. 497.

<u>America</u> thought Senator Bricker was carrying out an "overwrought campaign of intimidation".[18] The only moral issue, as <u>America</u> saw it was that:

> Clearly implicit in the Bricker Resolution are
> assumptions with which Catholics cannot agree.
> We cannot agree to the doctrine of the absolute
> sovereignty of national states. We cannot agree
> to a self centered nationalism as the over-all
> principle governing our foreign policies. We
> stand for cooperation with all members of the
> world community.[19]

<u>Commonweal</u> saw the Bricker Amendment simply as a test of Presidential power.

> If he [Eisenhower] went all the way with the views
> of some of the Republicans now in Congress, the
> President would still have a desk, a chair and
> office, but little else.[20]

Another article in <u>Commonweal</u> pointed out that the real issue in the Bricker proposal was the reluctance of Congress to accept U.N. standards of human rights in the U.S. In fact, it wrested the issue away from human rights and made the U.N. standards appear to be less than adequate to meet the American civil rights criterion.

---

[18]
"Legislation by Intimidations: The So-Called Bricker Resolution", <u>America</u>, July 4, 1953, p. 352
[19]
"Dulles vs. Bricker", <u>America</u>, April 13, 1953, p.69.

[20]
"End of the Road: Senator Bricker's Proposed Constitutional Amendment", <u>Commonweal</u>, August 7, 1953, p. 433.

> Senator Bricker has clearly stated the purpose of
> his resolution: 'I do not want any of the inter-
> national groups, and especially the group headed
> by Mrs. Eleanor Roosevelt, which has drafted the
> Covenant of 459 Human Rights to betray the funda-
> mental, inalienable and God-given rights of American
> citizens enjoyed under the Constitution. This is
> really what I am driving at'. 21

In April of 1953, the Catholic Association for International

Peace, which had sent an observer to the U.N. organizational

meeting in San Francisco and had worked for the inclusion of

Articles 55 and 56 as part of the U.N. Charter, finally issued a

statement in opposition to the Bricker Amendment.[22] While it

rejected the proposed law on the belief that the Bricker

resolution would undermine the public faith in the United States,

it made no specific mention of the fact that the Bricker

Amendment presented a threat to continued American human rights

policy initiated at the U.N. The text was inserted into the

Appendix of the Bricker Hearings but no other action was taken by

any Catholic organization to stop the Senator's attempt to end U.S.

international human rights policy based on treaty law.

III. The Seeds of American Catholic Integration, 1950-1965

A. Anti-Communism

Although the Bricker "compromise" set the course of United

States international human rights foreign policy for nearly

21
H.C. Hinton, "Bricker Amendment", Commonweal, August 15,
1952, p. 458.

22
See "The Bricker Resolution Restricting Conduct of United
States Foreign Relations", in Bricker Hearings, op. cit.,
pp. 1200-1201.

twenty years, the decision to give human rights a low priority in American foreign policy was also influenced by the overriding national preoccupation of the time: how to deal with the growing Communist threat. Because of this problem, neither the U.S. government, nor the American Catholic Church, viewed human rights as a major consideration in the development of U.S. foreign policy during the Cold War years. Ironically, however, Catholic support for government anti-Communist measures at home and abroad played a part in helping to integrate the Church both politically and socially in the U.S., and helped to establish a potential political situation in the 1970's by which the Church would be able to help in the development of a viable international human rights foreign policy in the future.

Catholicism had traditionally been the adversary of Communism. As early as 1846, two years before the publication of the Communist Manifesto, Pius IX had referred to the followers of Marxism as "hostile enemies...seized by a certain blind force of mad impiety"[23] who seek to deceive and delude Christians. In 1878, Pope Leo XIII, in Quod Apostolici Muneris, echoed his predecessor's opposition toward Communism. He wrote that it would "...defile the flesh", and that it was a "fatal plague which insinuates itself into the very marrow of human society

------

23
    Henricus Denzinger, ed., Enchiridion Symbolorum (Barcelonia: Herder, 1948), p. 455. Qui Pluribus, November 9, 1946.

only to bring about its ruin".[24]

In modern times, Pope Pius XI had led the Catholic fight against Communism, condemning it in many encyclicals, particularly Miserentissimus Redemptor,[25] Quadrogesimo Anno,[26] Caritate Christi,[27] Acerba Animi,[28] Delectissima Nobis,[29] and Divini Redemptoris.[30] In Divini Redemptoris, Leo contrasted the differences between the principles of Marx and those of Jesus. He argued that dialectical,historical materialism, constant class conflict, and the movement to a classless society only stressed man's role in attaining and accelerating perfection. Official Church condemnation of Communism resulted from the fact that it denigrated God, recognized no spirit, no soul, no after life or future escatalogical hope. In short, it

24
    John J. Wynne, ed., The Great Encyclical Letters of Pope Leo XIII (New York: Benzinger Brothers, 1903), pp. 22-23. Quod Apostolici Muneris, December 28, 1879.
25
    Acta Apostolica Sedis XX (1928): 165-168. Miserentissimus Redemptor. May 8, 1928.
26
    Acta Apostolica Sedis XXIII (1931) : 177-228. Quadrogesimo Anno. May 15, 1931.
27
    Acta Apostolica Sedis XXIV (1932): 177-194. Caritate Christi. May 3, 1932.
28
    Acta Apostolica Sedis XXIV (1932): 321-332. Acerba Animi. September 19, 1932.
29
    Acta Apostolica Sedis XXV (1933): 261-274. Delectissima Nobis. June 3, 1933.
30
    Acta Apostolica Sedis XXIX (1937): 65-106. Divini Redemptoris. March 19, 1937.

left no room for man's reliance on God. The Church accused Communism of denying individual liberty, vilifying man's personality and removing moral restraints, claiming that it made the individual a mere "cog-wheel" in the Communist system.[31]

Further, the Church opposed Communism because it used marriage and the family as artificial, civil institutions to establish a specific economic system. The matrimonial bond lost its juridical and moral status, according to the Church, and education as well as the care of the children fell to the collectivity. Finally, the withering away of the state and the dream of a classless society were castigated as goals obstructing man's striving for his ultimate escatological reward.

> Such Venerable Brethern is the new gospel which Bolshevik and atheistic Communism, offers the world as glad tidings of deliverance and salvation. It is a system full of errors and sophisms. It is in opposition both to reason and Divine Revelation. It subverts the social order, because it means the destruction of its foundations; because it ignores the true origin and purpose of the State; because it denies the rights of dignity and liberty of human personality. 32

This rejection of Communism, growing out of a tradition of respect for the dignity of the individual, became more pronounced as World War II began. American Catholics, as well as the

---

31
  Ibid., pp. 69-71.

32
  Ibid., p. 72.

Vatican, had opposed the U.S.-Soviet alliance, and as soon as the War ended, the American Catholic Bishops issued a statement calling for the government to reconsider its relations with the U.S.S.R. They publicly went on record in 1945 saying that:

> There are profound differences of thought and policy between Russia and the western democracies. Russia has acted unilaterally on many important settlements. It has sought to establish its sphere of influence in eastern and south eastern Europe, not on the basis of sound regional agreements in which sovereignties and rights are respected, but by the imposition of its sovereignty and by ruthlessly setting up helpless puppet states. Its Asiatic policy, so important for the peace of the world is an enigma...34

The Catholic Church was most aware of the Soviet consolidation of power in the immediate post-War period, having suffered the loss of many traditional Catholic nations to Communist aggression: Poland, Hungary, Czechoslovakia, Rumania, Albania, Bulgaria, Yugoslavia, East Germany, Estonia, Latvia, and Lithuania. Clergy had been decimated and hierarchy persecuted; most notably, Joseph Cardinal Mindzenty of Hungary, Archbishop Aloysius Stepinac of Yugoslavia, Archbishop Joseph Beran of Czechoslovakia and Archbishop Joseph Groesz of East Germany. Untold numbers of schools, hospitals and churches had been nationalized, and a systematic attack against Catholicism was

---

33
See Flynn, op.cit., Chapter 5, "Russia", pp.137-174.

34
Text of Bishops Statements, "On Peace and Reconstruction", New York Times, 18 November 1945, p. 28.

being waged successfully by the Communists in the aftermath of World War II.[35]

No surprise, then, when Whittaker Chambers accused Alger Hiss, a high ranking State Department official of being a Soviet spy in 1948, that American Catholics were easily swept into the post-War Communist paranoia. Their fears seemed substantiated, too, when the Vatican, in 1949, placed the ban of excommunication on any Catholic who belonged to the Communist party. The directive forbade enlisting in, or showing favor to, the Communist party; publishing, reading, or disseminating books, or other literature supporting Communism. It stated that only the Holy See could lift the ban of excommunication; that local officials could not.[36]

American Catholics continued to have their distrust of Communism reenforced during the post-War years: the fall of China in 1949, the invasion of Korea in 1950, the shock of the Klaus Fuchs scandal in the same year. At home, the U.S. was subject to Soviet subversion. In 1945, the F.B.I. found over 1,000 classified State Department documents in the offices of _Amerasia_, a publication sympathetic to the Communists.

35
    See Camille M. Cianfarra, _The Vatican and the Kremlin_, (New York: E.P. Dutton, 1950). Contains an analysis of methods and tactics used by the Communists to destroy religion in Eastern Europe and to create an atheistic state.

36
    Acta Apostolica Sedis XLI (1949): 334. _Decretum Suprema Sacra Congregatione_. July 1, 1949.

Accusations by ex-Communists Whittaker Chambers, Elizabeth Bently, Louis F. Budenz and Freda Utley, the latter three of whom happened to be converts to Catholicism, kept stoking the fires of American Catholic concern over domestic and international Communism.

The man who took these allegations, led the crusade to rid the government of Communists, and who most embodied the Red paranoia of the times was Senator Joseph McCarthy (R-Wisconsin). "Tail Gunner Joe" was, coincidentally, also a Catholic. Educated At Marquette University as an undergraduate,he also attended the University's law school. In 1950, facing re-election with no significant achievements during his first term as Senator, McCarthy was looking for an issue or a cause that would assure his re-election to the Senate in 1952. Historians are in disagreement as to how he arrived at the decision to use Communism to catapult him to national prominence. [*]

Some scholars claim that Father Edmund Walsh, S.J., of Georgetown University, gave him the idea, [37] although this has

---

[*]
Some writers such as WIlliam F. Buckley and Brent Bozell in McCarthy and His Enemies (Chicago: Henry Regnery, 1954), claimed that the State Department had not met its responsibilities to rid the government of Communists, especially in the Amerasia and Hiss cases. It was their contention that McCarthy did not "use" the Communist issue, but that he was merely doing what the State Department, itself, had failed to do.

[37]
Eric Goldman, The Crucial Decade--And After, (New York: Alfred A. Knopf, 1965, pp. 139-141). Goldman relies heavily on the allegations and private information of Drew Pearson and his associates.

never been substantiated. Others claim that another priest, Father Joseph Cronin, of the Social Action Department of the National Catholic Welfare Council, was supposed to have been the source of much of McCarthy's information used in his Communist allegations. Again, this does not seem verifiable.[39]

McCarthy, himself, attacked rampant Communism in the State Department, the Voice of America, the Army, the movie industry, and even the Churches. Such well known individuals as Owen Lattimore, Phillip Jessup, John Stewart Service, Henry Julian Wadleigh, Noel Field, Laurence Duggan, Harry Dexter White, Maurice Halperin and Dorothy Kenyon were accused by McCarthy of being Communists. He attacked, by inference, the reputations of General George C. Marshall, Adlai Stevenson, Professor Frederick Schumann and Dr. Harlow Shapely. McCarthy's frenzy did not subside, but was fed instead by the federal investigation, conviction, and execution of two Americans as Soviet spies in 1953, Ethel and Julius Rosenberg. Bouyed by the fear of Communism aroused by the sensational Rosenberg case, McCarthy continued to accuse others.

------

[38]
Donald F. Crosby, God, Church and Flag. Senator Joseph McCarthy and the Catholic Church 1950-1957, (Chapel Hill: University of No. Carolina Press, 1978, p. 52). He claims that "It is highly improbable...that Walsh urged McCarthy to go on a crusade against subversives..." He relies mainly on interviews with Walsh's colleagues; but Walsh,himself, never did make a public denial.

[39]
Ibid., p. 56. Crosby says that "McCarthy completely ignored their information..." Crosby's conclusion is based on interviews with Walsh's colleagues, but he has no definitive proof for his statement.

The attitude of many American Catholics toward McCarthy and his pursuit of Communists was one of approval. Although a significant minority opposed his tactics and actions, the Catholic press did not reflect this split accurately. Instead, it served as a forum to mirror the conservative views of the Catholic elite: editors of Catholic newspapers, the hierarchy,and Catholic interest groups. All were vying for mass Catholic support for their points of view.

> While Catholics were definitely split on the McCarthy issue, there was a preponderance of pro-McCarthy sentiment among Catholics. It may have been exaggerated or given undue emphasis, but it is clear from the available evidence that it predominated among Catholics who spoke out on the issue...some Catholics were reluctant to criticize McCarthy because he was Catholic. There was an affinity between them and the Senator on religious grounds...Then, there were many who believed that only Catholics fully understood the menace of Communism, an avowedly anti-religious movement...But much of McCarthy's Catholic support came from the essentially isolationist element of American Catholicism. McCarthy voiced the frustrations of this group... [F] or them he kept the problems small and the solutions simple and created the impression that all our worries would be over 'when the State department is cleaned out'. 40

Among the prominent Catholic periodicals, only Commonweal and America were opposed to McCarthy, his views, and methods. John Cogley, as the lay editor of Commonweal, had virtually a free hand to criticize Senator McCarthy, while Robert Hartnett, S.J., the Jesuit editor of America, did not. When Hartnett's

---

40
  Vincent De Santis, "American Catholics and McCarthyism", The Catholic Historical Review 2 (April, 1965): 29-31.

attacks had sufficiently irked his conservative superiors, he was directed (in May of 1954) to stop his criticism of Senator McCarthy. In 1955, Hartnett "retired" as editor of America.

Those periodicals which most favored McCarthy were the Brooklyn Tablet, The Boston Pilot, Ave Maria, Our Sunday Visitor and the (St. Paul) Wanderer. Articles in much of the Catholic press seemed to reflect greater Catholic support for McCarthy than actually existed. Vincent De Santis, who has done extensive work in this area, has gone back over the Gallup Poll surveys of the time and has reported that in 1950, 49% of Catholics favored the Senator, virtually the same percentage of Protestants who also supported him.[41] In 1953, that percentage rose to 51% and in 1954 it reached an all time high of 58%[42] However, never did Catholic support for McCarthy represent an overwhelming monolithic stance, as the Catholic press tried to indicate.

Catholic support for anti-Communism and Joseph McCarthy was expressed, however, by one of the most vocal members of the Catholic hierarchy, Francis Cardinal Spellman. In 1954, a clash between Spellman and Bishop Bernard J. Sheil of Chicago occurred over the Cardinal's blatant support for McCarthy.

_____

[41]
    Ibid, p. 2

[42]
    Ibid, p. 24.

When it appeared that McCarthy might be censured by the Senate for his behavior in his witch-hunt for subversives, Cardinal Spellman arranged a speaking engagement for him at a Communion Breakfast in New York City. Spellman had assembled a group of 6,000 sympthetic policemen who had obviously been invited in a show of Catholic support for the Senator. Four days later, however, Bishop Sheil armed with a speech written by John Cogley of Commonweal, addressed 2,500 members of the United Auto Workers who were meeting in Chicago at the time. Severely criticizing McCarthy, Sheil found himself, the next day, the object of criticism by much of the Catholic press. In September 1954, Sheil abruptly "resigned" too, as Director General of Chicago's Catholic Youth Organization (CYO).*

Some Catholic interest groups did seem to be in favor of McCarthy, particularly the Catholic War Veterans, the Knights of Columbus and the Association of Catholic Trade Unionists. However, none of these organizations was able to solidify support for its views and rally mass Catholic support to stave off the ultimate censure of Senator McCarthy. In late 1954, American support for McCarthy slipped from 58 to 56%[43] and both

---

*There is no direct evidence to show that Sheil was fired. It is interesting however, that Sheil's papers on this subject were either lost or burned as Crosby, op.cit., p. 169, has reported. Crosby was denied official permission to read the diocesan files on the Sheil case as late as 1978, the publication date of his book.

43
Ibid

the issue and the man continued to lose ground among Catholics.

Concern for Communism, however did have the ironic result of helping to integrate Catholics into the American mainstream during the Cold War years. The issue gave American Catholics an opportunity to reenforce their patriotism shown in World War II. Anti-Communism was true Americanism, and now anti-Communism was true Catholicism as well. Indeed, by the 1950's Americanism and Catholicism seemed to be made of the same ingredients.

The McCarthy phenomena:

> ...demonstrated that the religious and political convictions of American Catholics had become inextricably intertwined. Religious practice had become politicized and political beliefs had been elevated to the status of religious creed...In short, the McCarthy era brought about a renewal and an intensification of the civil religion. 44

From this point on, Catholics began to make social and political strides in the United States. As we shall see, they appeared to be less of a threat to the democratic system as they tried, themselves, to work with their former rivals, to reconcile their religious views with the American way of life, and to reform their own institutional inadequacies. American Catholicism was on its way to becoming an acceptable social and political force in the United States.

B. Better Inter-Faith Relations

44
  Crosby, op.cit., pp. 172-251.

By the decade of the 1950's, the long struggle between Catholics and Protestants for political, social and economic dominance in the United States began to ebb. Their intense interdenominational rivalry had begun after the Civil War with the massive influx of Catholic immigrants. They swelled the American population during the latter half of the 19th century, leading to keen competition for jobs,housing and education. The Catholic allegience to Rome was interpreted as a sign of their loyalty to the Pope rather than to the President, and it was understood by Protestants that good catholics could not also be good Americans. Conscious Catholic separatism led to a Protestant fear and distrust of their education goals and political aspirations. Catholics found themselves as the economic and social underclass during the 19th and into the 20th centuries. The Protestants did not want the Catholics to wrest any power, in any area, away from them. Religious squirmishes were commonplace; federal aid to Catholic schools, a U.S. Representative to the Vatican and the Presidential bid of Al Smith in 1928 were just a few of the recurring problems which continued to keep the Catholic-Protestant rivalry alive until after World War II. After that,however, the radicalism of the 19th and 20th centuries between both groups finally to started to dissipate, giving way to the more moderate voices on each side. Protestants like Reinhold Niebuhr, John C. Bennett, Robert McAfee Brown, John M. Krumm, and Jaroslav Pelikan initiated efforts at dialogue with Catholics. At the same time, George Tavard, John

J. Kane, Gustave Weigel, Robert F. Drinan, John Courtney Murray, and Walter Ong attempted a Catholic movement toward encounters with Protestants.

The reasons why better inter-faith relations began to develop at this time are quite complex. One explanation was offered by Will Herberg, an American Jew, who was an objective observer of the diminishing religious conflict. He had the insight to explain the embryonic cooperation between America's past religious rivals from a sociological point of view. It was Herberg's thesis in his classic work, Protestant--Catholic--Jew,[45] that an "American religion" had emerged during the course of American history, a "religion" whose "theology" helped to unify U.S. religious denominations. This religion, according to him, was "the American way of life", a belief in God, prayer and an after-life, operative within the framework and fundamentals of democracy. These principles included faith in individualism, dynamism, pragmatism, progress and education. Herbert contended that over many generations the secularization of Puritanism had occurred, culminating in the integration of Protestants, Catholics and Jews into a functional religious pluralism by the mid-twentieth century.

45
    See, Will Herberg, Protestant--Catholic--Jew, (New York: Doubleday, 1955).

Another explanation for the lessening of religious tension in America was offered by Winthrop Hudson of the Colgate-Rochester Divinity School. He claimed that a decline in Protestant influence had occured, due to the massive influx of Catholic immigrants to the cities, giving them more power over rural Protestants than their numbers would indicate.[46] He also thought that Protestant theology had eroded over the years, thus bringing about a Protestant religious complacency, and a Catholic acceptance by Protestants. Further, Hudson argued that American Protestantism could neither adjust to the challenge of Catholicism, nor to the new, scientific intellectual world. In short, Hudson claimed that fundamentalist Protestant beliefs could not cope with the changes of the American twentieth century.

Joseph H. Fichter, S.J., in a significant paper interpreted the dissipating Protestant-Catholic conflict in the 1950's, as the result of the Americanization of Catholicism.[47] This he saw as one of a number of more or less simultaneous and natural processes by which "Roman" Catholicism underwent socialization, accommodation and assimilation causing it to emerge as an "American" religious denomination. Fichter argued

---

46
    See Thomas McAvoy, ed., Roman Catholicism and the American Way of Life, (South Bend: Notre Dame Press, 1960), pp. 22-27.

47
    Ibid., pp. 113-127.

that during this process, the American Catholic Church was impacted by American culture, and that as a result "Roman" Catholicism began to lose its immigrant status, and take on many of the traits of the American way of life. These included co-operation and interaction, until finally, by mid century, both Protestants and Catholics accepted each other's behavior. This created a new behavior different from both. This phenomena, he believed, was religious pluralism, the outgrowth of the Americanization of Catholicism.

There were other factors, demographic, political, social and economic, which also led to a lessening of religious tension between Catholics and Protestants in America during the years 1950-1965. By mid-century, the Catholic demographic picture revealed a population which was predominatly native born. The restrictive immigration quotas of the 1920's which limited the influx of foreigners to the United States, did not slow down the burgeoning Catholic population. Although there were only 17,736,000 Catholics in America in 1920, most of whom were immigrants, the Catholic birth rate caused that number to soar to 27,766,000 in 1950. That number of mostly native born Catholics continued to climb to 42,105,000 in 1960, resulting in an almost doubling of the American born Catholic population in one decade.[48]

Andrew Greeley, in his sociological study, The American Catholic,[49]

---

[48]
See U.S. Census, op. cit., pp. 391-392.

[49]
Andrew Greeley, The American Catholic, (New York: Basic Books, 1977).

found that by the early 1960's Catholics had been absorbed into the American social, economic and political mainstream; that they had achieved educational and economic parity with Protestants. Indeed, Greeley's data also led him to claim that the American Catholic population was evolving into an independent collectivity. This meant that Catholics were becoming less receptive to Church influence; that Church control over the social, political and even religious thinking of its members was beginning to wane. A more secularized Catholic population, socially aware, politically concerned, and independent was beginning to emerge.

Politically, several events also helped to dissipate past Catholic-Protestant rivalry. The new President, Dwight Eisenhower, did not press immediately for the appointment of a representative to the Vatican after General Mark Clark withdrew his name for considerastion for that position in 1951. His decision to wait for a while before making any selection, provided time for the volatile feelings of both religious groups to subside. At the same time, no controversial Supreme Court decisions were handed down during the 1950's on questions of Church and State* significant enough to cause interdenominational strains as in the past. Further, the battle over federal aid to parochial schools was also put to rest during the decade.

----

* An exception was <u>Zorach</u> <u>vs.</u> <u>Clauson</u> in 1952. However, because it allowed for release time for religious education, it satisfied those who were opposed to religious teachers coming to the public schools as well as those who wanted their children to receive such instruction.

Socially, racial events also caused Catholic-Protestant tensions to wane. A new vocal minority, the Blacks, challenged both religious groups. In 1954, as a result of <u>Brown</u> <u>vs.</u> <u>Topeka</u>, the Supreme Court inadvertently changed the focus of inter-group tensions in the United States. The quest for school integration and Black civil rights shifted the spotlight from the religious conflict between Protestants and Catholics, and brought attention, instead, to the underlying struggle between Blacks and Whites. Minority groups were now realigned along racial, rather than religious lines.

The dynamic inter-play of all these factors, demographic, - political, economic and social, resulted in a diminishing of the Protestant-Catholic conflict in this country during the 1950's. By the end of the decade even some movement toward reconciliation could begin to be felt. In the late 1950's one of the most anti-Catholic organizations in the United States, Protestants and Other Americans United (POAU) found itself with a dwindling membership roster. The National Council of Churches also began to wane in its enthusiasm for the organization and in 1958, the Connecticut Council of Churches completely disavowed all POAU activities. Publication of <u>An</u> <u>American</u> <u>Dialogue</u> (suggested by Will Herberg), an inter-faith discussion between the Protestant, Robert McAfee Brown and the Catholic, Gustave Weigel, further encouraged the embryonic Catholic-Protestant encounter. Ecumenical meetings at Oberlin in 1957 and Belleville, Illinois

(Operation Understanding sponsored by the Catholic Bishops), also helped efforts at an inter-faith movement. Such encounters continued to proliferate as the decade drew to a close. In 1958, the private sector joined university and church efforts at ecumenism, when the Ford Foundation's "Fund for the Republic", sponsored a seminar on "Religion in a Free Society". Organized by John Cogley, past editor of Commonweal, the conference brought together the greatest American religious minds to ponder the question of Church and State in a free country.* Thus, the 1950's began a period of religious understanding and a time of wound healing. Indeed, the decade signaled the start of a functional religious pluralism in the United States. This further assimilation and acceptance of American Catholicism by Protestants became one more step on the way to creating a climate in which the Church would be able to participate in the process to help formulate American human rights foreign policy two decades hence. In fact, we shall see how, at that time, the Catholic Church worked in coalition with the Protestants, their former rivals, to influence the Congress on human rights matters.

---

*
See the publication of original papers on religious pluralism, Church and State, the School issue, the secular challenge and religion in a free society. John Cogley, ed., Religion in America, (New York: Meridan Books, 1958).

C. The Candidacy and Election of John Kennedy

The candidacy and election of John Kennedy also served to bring about the further integration and acceptance of Catholics into the American mainstream. It brought about a political catharsis in this country by putting the religious issue out in the open again, and forcing people to face their religious prejudices squarely. All the burgeoning inter-faith good will of the 1950's was put to the test when it became apparent that John Kennedy, the Catholic Senator from Massachusetts, was going to pursue the nomination of the Democratic Party for the Presidency in 1960.

Kennedy was not a likely candidate. He had no national following. He was neither a powerful political leader, although he served in both the House and the Senate; nor a military hero, although his courage had been demonstrated in the famous PT 109 incident in World War II. Like Al Smith, three decades earlier, he was both Irish and Catholic.

But there the similarities ended and his strengths as a candidate emerged: impeccable social and educational credentials, dedicated to humanistic, not dogmatic, religious principles,[50] an independent, ecumenical man.[51] As the son of a millionaire, who had been Ambassador to the Court of St. James,

---

[50]
See Nicholas Schneider, The Religious Views of President John J. Kennedy, (St. Louis: Herder, 1965).

[51]
See Lawrence H. Fuchs, John F. Kennedy and American Catholicism, (New York: Meredith Press, 1967).

John Kennedy had participated in the privileged Protestant world even though he was a Catholic. Except for one year in a Catholic school, Kennedy was educated at, and graduated from, both Choate and Harvard. He disavowed any ecclesiastical pressure in politics. He had not supported either the appointment of a representative to the Vatican, parochial aid to education, or foreign aid to Catholic Yugoslavia and Poland. Theodore Sorenson, Kennedy's Administrative Assistant for many years, and eventually Special Counsel to the President, assessed the future President's motives. He wrote: "He simply wanted to be President and happened to be Catholic".[52]

While Al Smith had never dealt effectively with the question of how he would reconcile his Catholic religious principles with the political demands of the American presidency, Kennedy realized that he would have to meet the issue head on early in the primaries. He had no opposition in the first one in New Hampshire, and in the second in Wisconsin against Hubert Humphrey the matter was minimized by both the candidates, if not the press. Having won both states, and adding Indiana as a third, the issue finally came out into the open in the fourth primary: West Virginia.

When Kennedy began campaigning there he tried to "offset the religious issue, he emphasized other issues, especially his

---

52
    Theodore Sorenson, _Kennedy_, (New York: Harper and Roe, 1965) p. 26.

efforts for the unemployed...." However, repeated newspaper surveys showed well over half of Humphrey's support was based solely on Kennedy's relgion.[54] Theodore H. White in his _Making of the President 1960_ noted: "The issue, it was clear was religion... it was to the candidate alone to decide...to attack-- he would meet the religious issue head on".[55]

Protestant clergymen came to Kennedy's aid during the West Virginia primary. Contacted by Ted Sorenson, the Very Reverend Francis B. Sayre, Jr., Dean of the Washington Episcopal Cathedral and the Methodist Bishop, G. Bromley Oxnam, a former leader of the POAU, led the drafting of an open letter to their fellow pastors urging tolerance and moderation in the primaries. These efforts and those of the candidate and his staff, secured victory in West Virginia and enough other primaries to assure Kennedy the nomination for the Presidency in 1960.

In September, right before the election, however, the whole issue of Catholicism and the Presidency blew up. At that time, a meeting was held in Washington, D.C. by concerned Protestant clergymen who feared the election of a Catholic as President.

---

[53] _Ibid._, p. 139.

[54] _Ibid._, p. 142.

[55] Theodore H. White, _The Making of the President_, 1960, (New York: Atheneum, 1961), p. 106.

Known as the National Conference of Citizens for Religious Freedom, the group, with the Reverend Norman Vincent Peale as its spokesman,* issued a policy statement on 7 September casting doubt on Kennedy's fitness for the Presidency. In it, the ministers essentially contended that Kennedy could be so influenced by his religious responsibilities to the Roman Catholic Church that he would not be able to discharge the duties of the President of the United State properly.

In a quick response, Kennedy decided to accept a previously offered invitation to address the Houston Ministerial Association on 12 September and bring the religious problem out into the open. Ted Sorenson, who helped write the speech, reported that:

> The Senator's desire was to state his position so clearly and comprehensively that no reasonable man could doubt his adherence to the Constitution....I read the speech over the telephone to the Rev. John Courtney Murray,S.J. ....On the plane to Houston, the speech, along with all possible questions that might follow from the floor, was also reviewed with both James Wine and his temporary aid, John Cogley...56

In Houston, Kennedy went on record as supporting the absolute separation of Church and State and, at the same time, he disavowed any and all ecclesiastical pressures on public officials. Calling for religious tolerance, he asked that private religious views, be discounted as a condition for holding

---

*

Peale withdrew from the organization very soon after its statement was made.
56
Sorenson, op. cit., p. 192.

public office. He asked to be judged on his fourteen year Congressional record. Most importantly, he pledged to make political decisions on the basis of the national interest, and promised to resign if his conscience and office were ever in conflict.

Most historians agree that the religious issue was dead after Houston. Schlesinger said that at Houston Kennedy "knocked religion out of the campaign as an intellectuallly respectable issue; it would persist, of course, as a stream of rancor underground".[57] Sam Rayburn, Speaker of the House was reported as having said that Kennedy "ate 'em blood raw".[58]

Sorenson's rememberance and assessment was that:

> The Houston confrontation did not end the religious controversy or silence the Senator's critics....It made unnecessary any further full-scale answer from the candidate, and Kennedy, while continuing to answer questions, never raised the subject again. It offered in one document all the answeres to all the questions any reasonable man could ask. It helped divide the citizens legitimately concerned about Kennedy's views from the fanatics who had condemned him from birth. 59

The election of Kennedy did not signal the start of cooperative religious pluralism in America, rather, it reflected the phenomena already in the process of development. The election of John Kennedy did much, however, to destroy the

---

57
  Schlesinger, op. cit.,p. 68.

58
  Ibid., p. 193.

59
  Ibid.

minority consciousness of the American Catholic population. Some

scholars even believe that Kennedy served as a catalyst to do

more to "blunt the ancient mutal hatred of Catholics and non-
Catholics than any American had done".[60] In any case, it is clear

that the candidacy and election of John Kennedy served generally

as one more factor to further integrate Catholics into the

American mainstream. It also helped to create a climate of

political acceptance that would help the Church later as it

attempted to become involved politically on behalf of

international human rights.

D. Vatican II

The walls of American religious conflict continued to tumble

with the convening of a General Council in Rome by Pope John

XXIII in 1962. This meeting, the first held since Vatican I

(1869-70), heralded the possibility of Church modernization and

liberalism. Its opening was anticipated by Catholics and non-

Catholics alike as a momentus event.

President Kennedy wrote to the Pontiff:

> We hope that the Council will be able to present
> in clear and persuasive language effective
> solutions to the many problems confronting all
> of us and, more specifically, that is decisions
> will significantly advance the cause of inter-
> national peace and understanding. [61]

60
Lawrence H. Fuchs, John F. Kennedy and American
Catholicism, (New York: Meredith Press, 1967), p. 31.

61
Schneider, op. cit., p. 68. Letter of President to Pope
John XXIII, October 5, 1962.

Called by Pope John in 1959 for the purpose of aggiornamento, the Council was to work for the internal reform and renewal of the Church. However, by the time the Council was actually convened in 1962, it was clear that the Council also intended to reassess the external relationship of the Church with the rest of the world, as well. One group at the Council, particularly older Italian Cardinals associated with the Curia,* interpreted all problems in terms of non-historical, abstract principles. That is, they supported an unchanging orthodoxy suspended in time. A second group of international hierarchy and periti, theology experts, saw dogma as having to be responsive to modern problems. That is, they stressed the formulation of a theology alive to, and formed by, history and circumstance.[62]

The Council lasted for three years, from 1962 to 1965. During that time, the Church opened discussion into many matters of doctrine, reorganization, and inter-faith relations. Although the Council issued a total of sixteen decrees on these and other diverse subjects, for the purpose of this study, five statements are most significant: Lumen Gentium, also known as De Ecclesia (The Dogmatic Constitution of the Church), Gaudium et Spes (The Pastoral Constitution of the Church in the Modern World), Christus Dominus (The Decree on the Bishops' Pastoral Office in the Church),Unitatis Reintegratio (The Decree on Ecumenism), and Dignitatis Humanae (The Declaration on Religious Freedom).

---

*
The Civil Service of the Church.
62
For a detailed discussion of these philosophical outlooks see: Michael Novak, The Open Church, (New York: Macmillan, 1964), particularly Chapter 5.

The first three documents focused on the nature and mission of the Church, and changes within its institutional structure. The latter two stressed ecumenism and religious freedom. Taken together, all these matters distinctly influenced the status and functioning of the American Catholic Church within contemporary democracy and religious pluralism.

With the formulation of _Lumen Gentium_ and _Gaudium et Spes_, The Council set about to redefine the role and relationship of the Church to man and the world. The thrust of these two documents was to stress the Church's role as servant of mankind: "to foster brotherhood", "to give witness to the truth, to rescue and not sit in judgement, to serve and not be served."[63]

While emphasizing its traditional belief in the dignity and worth of man, the Council reflected on the changes and imbalances in the world. It noted the greater interdependence of men and nations and it affirmed the need for equality and social justice. Consequently, the Council supported all individuals in their quest for freedom and dignity, for human rights.

> ...the Church proclaims the rights of man.
> She acknowledges and greatly esteems the
> dynamic movements of today by which these
> rights are everywhere fostered. 64

Thus, the entire Catholic Church, in Council, went on record

63
Walter M. Abbott, gen. ed., _The Documents of Vatican II_, (New York: Herder and Herder, 1966), p. 201. _Gaudium et Spes_, Section 3.

64
Ibid., p. 241. _Lumen Gentium_, Section 41.

in support of attempts to secure human rights. However, at the same time, it cautiously stated:

> Christ, to be sure, gave his Church no
> proper mission in the political, economic
> or social order. The purpose he set before
> her is a religious one. 65

Thus, instead of actively participating in the political order to help men to attain their rights, the Church preferred to define its role as one of service to "consolidate the human community through Divine Law".[66]

Envisioning the Church's function as one of promoting unity, the Council stressed marriage and the family, and supported the development of a more human culture in which the economic and political order were to serve man.[67] While Vatican II encouraged human rights, in essence it gave no specific guidelines by which the Church should proceed in the future to make human rights a reality. Yet, the consequences of such an omission were not catastrophic. Instead the Church moved at a different rate and in various ways on human rights throughout the world in the years immediately following the Council.

With regard to politics, the Council stressed the autonomy of the Church and its need to co-operate with government.

65
  Ibid., p. 241, Section 42.

66
  Ibid.

67
  Ibid., pp. 241-185, Sections 42-75.

The role and competence of the Church being
what it is, she must in no way be confused
with the political community, nor be bound
to any political system. For she is at once,
a sign and a safeguard of the transcendence
of the human person.
In their proper spheres, the political
community and the Church are mutually independent and self-governing. Yet, by a
different title, each serves the personal
and social vocation of the same human beings.
This service can be more effectively rendered
for the good of all, if each works better for
wholesome mutual cooperation, depending on
the circumstances of time and place....[The
Church] does not lodge her hope in privileges
conferred by civil authority. Indeed, she
stands ready to renounce the exercise of
certain legitimately acquired rights if it
becomes clear that their use raises doubt
about the sincerity of her witness or that
new conditions of life demand some other
arrangement. 68

Thus, Vatican II reflected a co-operative attitude of the

Catholic Church toward the State. The Council agreed that the

contingencies of time and place and circumstance had to play a

role in determining how the Church should interact with the State

for the benefit of mankind. The Church was even willing to give

up rights, as well as privileges, if such positions compromised

the proper functioning of the Church in a changing world. As a

result of Vatican II, the Council articulated the belief that the

Church had to adapt its doctrines to the political realities of

the present.

68
    Ibid., pp. 287-288, Section 76.

In the area of internal renewal and reform, Vatican II made the most significant change. First, through _Lumen Gentium,_ _Gaudium_ et _Spes_ _and_ _Christus_ _Dominus_, the Council took broad measures to modernize the Roman-oriented structure of the Church and to define the role of the Bishops in its government. Second, in _Unitatis_ _Reintegratio_ and _Dignitatis_ _Humanae_, the Church stressed the need for ecumenism and religious freedom.

In an effort to reorganize the apparatus of the Church, the Bishops called for a change in the Curia while reasserting their own episcopal authority. Having been established in 1588 as the civil service of the Church, the Curia had actually degenerated into a bureaucratic maze of interlocking directorates over the centuries. Nourished by patronage, staffed by Italian conservative Cardinals (usually cronies of the Popes), it had the power to influence the Pontiff, and in turn, the policies of the Church. The Bishops called for an end to such an antiquated, one-sided, form of internal government.

> In exercising supreme, full, and immediate power over the universal Church, the Roman Pontiff makes use of the departments of the Roman Curia....The Fathers of this most sacred Council, however, strongly desire that these departments...be reorganized and better adapted to the needs of the times, and of various regions and rites. This task should give special thought to their number, name, competence and particular method of procedure as well as to the coordination of their activities. The Fathers also eagerly desire that...the office of legate...be more precisely determined...be drawn more widely from

various geographical areas of the Church...
[be filled with] diocesan [bishops]...
[and] give a greater hearing to laymen... 69

While the Bishops emphasized the modernization and de-Romanization of the Curia, they stressed their own authority as well. Within the institutional hierarchy they saw themselves as assistants to the Pope having the responsibility for the government of the universal Church.[70] In their own dioceses,however, the Bishops envisioned their main role as one of service: to teach, sanctify and govern. With regard to each other, the Bishops stressed filial cooperation and declared: "This sacred Ecumenical Synod earnestly desires that the venerable institution of synods and councils flourish with new vigor".[71] Further, the Bishops declared that they intended to unite regionally, and to establish associations to work for the common good.[72] Thus, they established the precedent to set up the machinery to act in concert, free of Curial interference, and with authority, on timely matters in their areas of the world. We shall see later how this affected the reorganization and functioning of the American Bishops and the NCWC after 1966.

---

[69]
   Ibid., pp. 401-403. Christus Dominus. Sections 9 and 10.

[70]
   Ibid., p. 400. Section 5

[71]
   Ibid., p. 424. Section 36.

[72]
   Ibid., p. 425, Section 37.

The Council also dealt with ecumenism and religious freedom. Both these matters were significant to the American Catholic Church, an institution born in an alien religious climate and maturing within a system of religious pluralism. The main architects of the document on ecumenism and religious freedom were the Americans, Father Gustave Weigel, S.J. and Father John Courtney Murray, S.J. Important from the American point of view, these documents represented an attitude of cooperation and tolerance: the very premises of democracy and religious pluralism.

In *Unitatis Reintegration*, the Church made a sincere effort to heal the long standing breach between Catholicism and Protestantism. Admitting that "men of both sides were to blame"[73], the Council recognized all baptized men as brothers, finally accepting the fact that all Christian churches play an important role in salvation.[74] The Council also stressed the importance of eliminating the causes of Catholic-Protestant separation by

---

*

Unfortunately, father Weigel did not live to see the effects of his work, as he died between the 2nd and 3rd session of Vatican II.

73
Ibid., p. 345. *Unitatis Reintegratio*. Section 3.

74
Ibid., p. 346. Section 3.

supporting dialogue, renewal and reform. Further, it suggested
that Catholics take the first steps to help bring about religious
unity by changing their attitudes.[76] In short, the Council did
not want Catholic religious beliefs to become obstacles to inter-
faith cooperation.[77]

Indeed, Catholic theology appeared to be catching up with
the phenomena of American religious pluralism. Reenforced by the
passage of _Dignitatis Humanae_, the declaration of religious
freedom was the culmination of the life-time effort of John
Courtney Murray to "theologize" the constitutional principle of
freedom of conscience.

Dignitatis Humanae stressed three levels of religious
freedom: ethical, political and theological. On an ethical
plane, religious freedom was to be conceived as an inalienable
human right. On a political level, it was to be understood as a
right worthy of preservation and protection by government. On a
theological level, it was to be considered as the right which
justified the judicial freedom of the Church. The Bishops,
through Murray's document, agreed that:

---

[75]
Ibid., p. 347. Section 4.

[76]
Ibid., p. 348 and 351. Sections 4 and 7.

[77]
Ibid., p. 354. Section 11.

This Vatican Synod declares that the human
person has a right to religious freedom.
This freedom means that all men are to be
immune from coercion on the part of individuals or of social groups and of any human
power, in such ways that in matters religious
no one is to be forced to act in a manner
contrary to his own beliefs. Nor is anyone
to be restrained from acting in accordance
with his own beliefs, whether privately or
or publicly, whether alone or in association
with others, within due limits....This right
of the human person to religious freedom is
to be recognized in the constitutional law
whereby society is governed. Thus it is to
become a civil right. 78

Shifting the emphasis in religious tolerance from an
attitude of expediency to one of genuine respect for the moral
convictions of others occurred at Vatican II. Again, the Council
seemed to have confirmed the significance of the American ideal
of religious freedom.

What then did Vatican II accomplish which had a bearing on
America at mid-Century? In reassessing the role and nature of
the Church with regard to modern man, contemporary politics and
current social problems, Vatican II redefined the Church as
servant, not master; as unifier, not separator. But, most
importantly, Vatican II promulgated principles which had the
effect of reconciling American Catholic religious and political
beliefs. It supported and affirmed the American ideals of
democracy: belief in the worth and dignity of man, separation of
Church and State, support of human rights, adherence to freedom
of conscience and respect for religious diversity. The

78
   Ibid., pp. 678-679. Dignitatis Humanae. Section 2.

significance of such a turn of events cannot be overestimated. Since Catholic dogma finally mirrored American constitutional principles, non-Catholics no longer had reason to fear Catholics politically. The political integration of Catholics, begun during the Kennedy years, could continue and accelerate with renewed vigor.

At the same time, the intense introspection of the Council also led to internal reforms and changes of attitude within the Church which reflected the fact that the Church was willing to recognize itself as one religion among many, an equal partner in the salvation of men's souls. Calling for the end of social and religious separation, it pointed out that the Church no longer sought privileged status or governmental favor. It urged dialogue and ecumenism. It called for de-Romanization. It stressed the social concern of the Bishops. By emphasizing the institutional interests of the Church, it paved the way for Church involvement on behalf of international human rights. As a result of Vatican II, Catholic religious and social integration, also begun in the 1950's, continued to occur with increasing speed soon after the Council had completed its work. Thus, Vatican II also played a significant role in bringing about the political, social and religious integration of Catholicism in America.

IV. Conclusion

Looking back over the Cold War years, the compromise of the Eisenhower Administration in the controversy over the Bricker Amendment effectively ended any legally binding attempts by the U.S. to support human rights abroad. That policy persisted for nearly twenty years, and the lack of official Catholic opposition to such a policy of human rights gave silent Church approval to government complacency in the matter.

Other priorities replaced human rights as a significant factor in American foreign policy during the 1950's and early 1960's, particularly the question of how to respond to the growing threat of Communism. It was ironic that, as the government and the Church both allied against their common foe, better Church-State relations evolved. The support of the Church for government policies of anti-Communism, helped to integrate Catholics into the American mainstream, showing them to be patriotic and part of a new nativistic vanguard.

The Cold War years also saw other events occurring which helped to integrate Catholics politically, religiously and socially into the American way of life. Better inter-faith relations developed in the 1950's as a result of the inter-play of complex sociological factors: the growth of a native Catholic population, the evolution of religious pluralism, the Americanization of Catholicism, and the decline of Protestantism.

Catholic religious integration began. At the same time, Catholic political acceptance also occurred. The election of John Kennedy reflected Catholic political integration and helped to destroy the minority consciousness of American Catholics. Finally, Vatican II reenforced and helped to accelerate the total integration of Catholics into the American mainstream. It reconciled Catholic religious and political beliefs according to American constitutional principles. It urged religious cooperation and understanding. It stressed the social and charitable role of the Church.

Thus, by the mid-1960's, the American Catholic Church was no longer an alien, aggressive adversary within the United States. Instead, as an accepted and respected religious institution within America, it now had the potential to be a significant moral force in the American social and political arena. Indeed, the next Chapter will examine one aspect of the moral-political challenge of the American Catholic Church in the 1970's: the role of the American Catholic Church in the formulation of U.S. human rights foreign policy.

CHAPTER IV: RENEWED GOVERNMENT AND CHURCH
CONCERN FOR HUMAN RIGHTS, 1965-1978

I. Introduction

This chapter will ask two questions. First, why did American Catholic concern for human rights re-emerge in the late 1960's, and how did the Church manifest that interest? Second, why did U.S. government concern for human rights reawaken in the early 1970's, and how did an American foreign policy based on human rights evolve during that decade? In response to the first question, it can be said that renewed American Catholic concern for human rights developed as a result of government repression directed against the Church in Latin America. This occured because the Church challenged the tyrannical governments of both the Left and the Right during the 1960's. Its religious leaders and adherents were suppressed and eventually other secular political opponents were persecuted as well. The Latin American hierarchy and clergy, painfully aware of the human rights violations on their continent, sought ways to reveal and redress those abuses. Many spoke out at home and were punished. Many others turned for help and solidarity to the United States Episcopate, embodied after Vatican II in the National Council of Catholic Bishops (NCCB), and its advisory staff, the United States Catholic Conference (USCC). With their assistance, early attempts were made to publicize religious and political repression in Latin America. Later, in 1970, the USCC in coalition with the National Council of Churches (NCC), brought international attention to human rights violations in Latin America when both organizations publicly accused Brazil of such abuses before the Organization of American States (OAS). From that time on, the American Catholic Church became involved actively in the cause of international human rights and attempted to play a role in encouraging the U.S. government to incorporate human rights into the foreign policy decision making process.

U.S. government concern for human rights reawoke in the 1970's shortly after the OAS case, when in 1973, the first United States Congressional hearings on human rights were held. The Subcommittee on International Organizations and Movements of the House of Representatives, chaired by Rep. Donald Fraser of Minnesota, called together representatives of various non-governmental organizations and government personnel. Jointly, both groups discussed human rights violations openly, and tried to assess the implications of such repression for U.S. foreign policy. As a result of these hearings, over 150 additional hearings during the years 1973-1978, the Fraser Committee became the first governmental body to suggest officially that human rights be considered a significant factor in the development and practice of U.S. foreign policy, and to initiate legislation to that end. Within that five year period, Congress tied human rights to foreign aid, limiting economic and military assistance to those nations which consistently violated human rights. Later, a series of acts, known as the Harkin Amendments, further restricted the dispersal of funds from international fiscal institutions to such nations. By 1974, an office of Human Rights and Humanitarian Affairs was established and became part of the intrastructure of the U.S. State Department. In 1975, human rights gained in importance after the adoption of the Helsinki Accords, and in that same year the Jackson-Vanik Amendment attempted to tie trade to human rights.

These efforts were finally given executive support in 1977, when the new President, Jimmy Carter, sent a message to the Congress about foreign assistance within months of taking office. He told the members of that body that "We are now reforming the policies which have on occasion awarded liberal grants and loans to repressive regimens which violate human rights".[1] In May, of the first year of his administration, the President announced at the Notre Dame graduation that:

> The world is still divided by ideological
> disputes, dominated by regional conflicts,
> and threatened by [the] danger that we will
> not resolve the differences of race and
> wealth without violence or without drawing
> into combat major military powers. We can
> no longer separate the traditional issues
> of war and peace from the new global questions
> of justice, equity, and human rights.

---

[1]
Message of the President to Congress, March 17, 1977. See Weekly Compilation of Presidential Documents, Vol. 13, No.12 (Washington: United States Government Printing Office, 1977), p. 405.

It is a new world--but America should
not fear it. It is a new world--and we
should help to shape it. It is a new world
that calls for a new American foreign policy
--a policy based on constant defense in its
values and on optimism in our historical
view....[W]e have reaffirmed America's commitment to human rights as a fundamental tenet
of our foreign policy....We want the world
to know that our Nation stands for more than
financial prosperity....I understand fully
the limits of moral suasion....Nonetheless,
we can already see dramatic, world wide advances
in the protection of the individual from the
arbitrary power of the state. For us to ignore
this trend would be to lose influence and moral
authority in the world. To lead it will be to
regain the moral stature we once had....
Throughout the world today, in free nations and
in totalitarian countries as well, there is a
preoccupation with the subject of human freedom,
human rights. And I believe that it is incumbant
on us in this country to keep that discussion,
that debate, that contention alive. 2

The journey from complacency to a renewed and more committed

concern for international human rights by both the American

Catholic Church and the U.S. government is a complex, but

important story. The role played by the American Catholic Church

in helping the U.S. government to adopt such a posture was at

times indirect and limited, but positive nonetheless.

The potential for such a role had been evolving during the

post-War and Cold War years. Refugee work by the Church,

involvement in United Nations' human rights activities, and a

more liberal Church-State theory opened the door to better

2
Address of President Carter to the Graduates of Notre Dame
University, May 22, 1977. See Weekly Compilation of Presidential
Documents, Vol. 13, No.22 (Washington: United States Government
Printing Office, 1977), pp. 775-6.

Catholic-government relations. Coupled with those factors that helped to integrate Catholics into the American mainstream during the late 1950's and 1960's, the development of religious pluralism, the emergence of a significant native population, the Americanization of the Church, the declining Protestant rivalry, ecumenism fostered by Vatican II and the election of John Kennedy, placed the Catholic Church in a position to play a credible, influential role in the development of a government foreign policy based on consideration for human rights in the 1970's. Such a policy emerged during that decade and more humane and civilized criteria were at the center of U.S. foreign aid and trade commitments than ever before. Indeed, the human interest began to become equated with the national interest during the 1970's.

II. Renewed American Catholic Concern for Human Rights
     A. The Latin American Connection

The renewed concern for international human rights in the late 1960's and 1970's can be viewed either as an east-west, or north-south phenomena. The Catholic Church had been involved in the east-west international human rights conflict during the post war years, primarily in its defense of religious freedom in Communist dominated East Europe and Asia. In the late 1960's, however, the focus of religious freedom shifted to Latin America, where governmental suppression of human rights had become so blatant, that the Church, renewed by Vatican II, chose to involve itself, not only in the fight for religious freedom, but in the struggle for the economic, social and political independence of its members as well.

Latin America during the 1960's was a patchwork of many unstable political systems. On that continent every kind of government within the political spectrum could be found, from Communists on the far left, to military juntas on the right. Tentative, short-lived coalitions among the significant power groups, namely the landowners, the military, the labor unions, the political parties and the Catholic Church, were the political practice of the decade.[3] In fact, coup d'etats (golpes) seemed more common than elections.

North American concern for its southern neighbor was ambiguous. On the one hand, the U.S. government professed to be an equal partner with Latin America, and showed its sincerity by participating in the Organization of American States. On the other hand, a traditional paternalism still pervaded U.S.-Latin American foreign policy as evidenced by U.S. intervention at the Bay of Pigs in 1961, and the Dominican Republic in 1965. In 1969, Nelson Rockefeller was sent to Latin America by President Richard Nixon to reassess this equivocal foreign policy stance.

3
    Robert Tomasek, ed., Latin American Policies, (New York: Doubleday, 1970). See specifically, "The Latin American Political System", Charles W. Anderson, pp. 4-36.

Rockefeller's report claimed that the U.S. had allowed its special relationship with the Western Hemisphere to "deteriorate badly",[4] and made recommendations to "reinvigorate and re-shape our special relationship".[5] Essentially, Rockefeller called on the U.S. government to preserve freedom in Latin America by taking actions to insure political order, and to improve the quality of life there by helping to bring about social change. However, Rockefeller believed that political stability in Latin American could be achieved mainly by U.S. support of strong military governments, internal security agencies, and police training. Indeed, when he was questioned by members of the Senate about his findings and challenged to show that U.S. military assistance would not be used to impede social progress in Latin America, he stated:

> The U.S. must realize that political evolution
> is a lengthy process and that short term
> abberations should not be permitted to under-
> mine its long range commitments. Individual
> cases should be judged on their own merits....
> The problem of security in the Western Hemisphere
> is a serious one. For this reason, I believe
> that military assistance should be increased
> and that current restrictions....be modified
> to permit military sales...6

4
U.S., Congress, Senate, Subcommittee on Western Hemisphere Affairs of the Committee on Foreign Relations, Rockefeller Report on Latin America. 91st Cong., 1st sess., November 21, 1969, p.73.
5
Ibid., p. 74.
6
U.S., Congress, House, Subcommittee on Inter-American Affairs of the Committee on Foreign Affairs. Governor Rockefeller's Report on Latin America, 91st Cong., 1st sess., 1969, pp. 32-33.

Rockefeller called for increased U.S. expenditures for education, housing, health, and conservation, and mentioned only one _institution_ among all the forces of progress within society[*] as able to lead the change in Latin America: the Catholic Church. Yet he made no recommendations for U.S. support of that organization in its efforts on behalf of human rights or its attempts to raise the quality of life in Latin America.

The underlying assumption of the Rockefeller Report was, of course, that strong military governments alone could provide the conditions within which social progress would occur. It also assumed that the forces for change within society could advance by themselves without some sort of centralized Latin American institutional leadership. Both notions proved to be false. Indeed, where military governments had taken over in South America during the 1960's, repressive measures to maintain "order" were commonplace. In those situations, "order" had degenerated to virtually unquestioned government action and control. At the same time, a lack of consensus as to the political, social and economic goals of the continent among the power groups, as well as a lack of leadership among them, mitigated against true social progress in Latin America during the 1960's.

---

* He specifically singled out communications, science and technology, population growth, organization, nationalism, youth, labor, the military and business. Communism was mentioned as a violent force for change, but the essential reason for the need for increased security in Latin America.

103

A case in point is Brazil. During the decade of the 1960's four significant changes of government occurred. Juscelino Kubitscheck was replaced by Joao Goulart in 1961. The latter was overthrown in a "golpe" by General Humberto Castelo Branco in 1964. In 1967, General Artur Costa e Silva succeeded to the Presidency, and in 1969, General Emilo Garrastazu Medici came to power. Beginning in 1965, (during the rule of a strong military government) steps to insure political "order" were begun. In February of that year, state police and security agencies were taken over by the Federal Government. In October, all political parties were dissolved. By 1967, the President was given the right to declare a state of emergency and institute martial law without the consent of the Congress. Shortly thereafter, the military was given the right (by the National Security Law) to interpret government opposition as treason. In March 1968, the Congress was dissolved. And in December of that same year, the infamous Institutional Act No. 5 was decreed. It allowed the President to recess the government for any reason, not necessarily an emergency, suspend political rights, confiscate property and take over States and municipalities. In September 1969, "psychological", "revolutionary", or "subversive" warfare were made punishable by death, a penalty that had not existed previously in Brazil. One month later, a new Constitution virtually removed all limitations on the President's power.

Little social progress could or did occur within such a political milieu. Those who opposed or appeared to oppose such governmental activity were imprisoned, tortured, kidnapped and often killed. This information was not widely known due to self censorship by the Brazilian press and varying degrees of governmental control.[7]

During this period of upheaval, the chief opponent of the government's tyrannical policies in Brazil was the Catholic Church. Each newly formed government, in turn, had courted the Church for its powerful support. However, the Church often balked at legitimizing these regimes because, since Vatican II, it had begun to question its traditional marriage to the forces of stability. Instead, the Catholic Church in Brazil and much of Latin America began to see itself as a significant force for social change. In fact, one scholar contends that "the most striking aspect of Latin American Catholicism in the mid-twentieth century has been its new alignment behind popular demands for a better life in the secular sphere".[8]

In response to the principles expounded in Christus Dominus at Vatican II, the six hundred Latin American Bishops, in 1966, called for a reorganization of their episcopal conference, CELAM. In two important meetings after Vatican II, one at Mar del Plata in 1966, and another at Medellin in 1968, the Bishops, through

---

7
"Terror in Brazil, A Dossier", American Committee for Information on Brazil, April 1970, p. 1.

8
Frederick C. Turner, Catholicism and Political Development in Latin America. (Chapel Hill: University of North Carolina Press, 1971), p.3.

CELAM, commited themselves to advance human rights, and to restructure the Latin American political order, not on the principles of either the left or the right, but on the social magisterium of the Church.

The progressive hierarchy in Brazil, most notably Eugenio Cardinal Sales, Agnelo Cardinal Rossi, Monsignor Dom Helder Camara (Archbishop of Olina-Recife), Paul Cardinal Arns, Monsignor Jorge Marcos de Oliveira of Santo Andre and Monsignor Antonio Batista Fragoso (Bishop of Crateus) opposed the successive military regimes in their country during the 1960's. Their efforts were augmented by Father Fernado Bastos de Avila, S.J. of the Catholic University in Rio de Janiero associated with _Sintese_, a progressive Journal, Father Paul Crespo S.J., for his work with labor, and Father Henrique C. de Lima Vaz, S.J., a radical political activist.

By 1968, Dom Helder Camara had already called for a "structural revolution"[9] in Brazil, and soon became the most outspoken voice of protest against human rights violations occurring within his country. In the next year, 1969, the Brazilian Episcopate joined together to denounce the infamous Institutional Act #5 which had curtailed most civil rights in that country. The hierarchy publicly stated its opposition.

---

[9]
Dom Helder Camara, "La Violencia: Pocion Unica?" trans. Paul E. Sigmund, _Models of Political Change in Latin America_ (New York: Praeger, 1970), pp. 146-149.

We are determined to apply the principles
of the Second Vatican Council, of the
social encyclicals, and now of the Second
General Conference of the Latin American
Episcopate at Medellin. Even if this
causes us bitter personal difficulties, for
this is our response to the request of the
Holy Father, the needs of our people, and
to the outcry of civilization.
The present situation, given institutional form since last December, is an open
invitation to arbitrary action and the
violation of fundamental rights, such as
the right of defense and the right of the
legitimate expression of thought and
information. Power has been established in
a way that makes it very difficult to have
an authentic dialogue between governors and
governed and leads many Brazilians to
dangerous underground activity. 10

It was the Brazilian Bishops, then, which began to lead the
resistance against the governmental repression in Brazil.
Consequently, the clergy and activists suffered the most
persecution. Even Dom Helder Camara's assistant, Dom Henrique
Neto, was assassinated for his beliefs on non-violence, human
rights, and social justice.

Because the Church was at the center of opposition to
governmental abuses in Brazil, the hierarchy had first hand
information from its clergy and missionaries as to the actual
human rights violations occurring within that country. By 1968
and 1969, that information was being passed to the International
Commission of Jurists, Amnesty International, the Vatican, and
the Latin American Division of the United States Catholic

10
    Declaration of the Central Committee of the Brazilian
Episcopate, February 18, 1969, trans. Sigmund, op cit., p.152.

Conference (USCC). Protestant missionaries were sending similar reports to the National Council of Churches (NCC). Both Father Louis Colonnese, who headed the Latin American Division of the USCC from 1968-1971, and the Reverend William Wipfler, who was in charge of the Latin American Bureau of the NCC during the last part of 1960's and early 1970's claimed that the Brazilian Catholic hierarchy was frustrated by its poorly received attempts to bring the plight of the repression in their country to the attention of U.S. government. Indeed, Wipfler felt that U.S. support of militarism, aid for internal security and police training, coupled with the findings of the Rockefeller study, were in fact, perceived by the Brazilian hierarchy as a root cause of repression in that country.[11] Rejecting official U.S. government channels, then, the Brazilian hierarchy and clergy sought assistance from two segments of American society which they believed might be sensitive to their plight: academia and religion.[12] Both groups were active in the anti-Viet Nam War movement, were sensitive to oppression, and had already established an informal network of communications and coalitions to deal with matters opposed to official government policy.

---

[11]
Interview with Reverend William Wipfler, January 14, 1980.

[12]
Ibid.

Father Colonnese reported that prior to his appointment as head of the Latin American Division at the USCC (1968), letters, plus affidavits of kidnapping and torture began to be sent, first as a trickle, then in a flood to that department. On taking charge, Colonnese began a system of advocacy or intervention, on behalf of specific cases of human rights violations in Brazil which operated for about one and one half years from 1968-1969.[13] He claimed:

> It was an attempt to move information rapidly throughout the Americas--especially when that information might result in some collective action (political pressure, etc.) which could serve the human rights of individuals or groups. Example: when someone was unjustly imprisoned in a country, we would disseminate that information rapidly throughout the hemisphere and Europe. We would urge a particular response. For example, to send cables and letters to the minister of that country protesting the arrest and urging liberty for the prisoner. It worked! (on certain occasions).
>   After about one year many members realized they weren't getting the mailings or they piled up for a period of time (thus reducing the effectiveness of the program). We utilized cables for a while but the expense became prohibitive. [14]

Father Colonnese had been involved in Latin American affairs before his appointment as Director of Latin American affairs at the USCC. In 1963, he and Reverend John Considine and Monsignor William Quinn, had founded the Catholic Inter-American

---

13
Correspondence with Father Louis Colonnese, Oct. 29, 1980.

14
Ibid.

Cooperation Program (CICOP), to provide a platform for those Latin American clergy who wanted to be heard.[15] This was accomplished by holding a series of major meetings in the United States each year for the ten years of CICOP's existence. Here, a network of people familiar with, and concerned about, Latin America could meet annually, exchange economic, social and political data, discuss strategies to redress repression, and try to bring such persecution to light. Colonnese, Quinn and Considine also believed that CICOP should be ecumenical and open to all parties interested in Latin America. Protestant organizations were invited to attend, particularly the National Council of Churches. Reverend Wipfler recalled that Protestant participation began as early as 1965, at the Second CICOP Conference held in Chicago.[16] Over the years, members of the NCC were also invited to address that organization, and contacts between the NCC and the USCC (since Father Colonnese served as director of the Latin American Division of the USCC and CICOP), developed. A close working relationship between American Catholics and Protestants emerged in the area of human rights, too, in light of the emphasis of Vatican II on ecumenical interaction and support of regional, social concerns.

15
  Ibid.

16
  Conversation with Reverend Wipfler, Oct. 1980.

B. American Catholic Action to Develop an American
    Human Rights Constituency

In 1969, the American Catholic Church began to play a more active role in trying to create an American constituency concerned for international human rights, particularly in Latin America. In that year, the CICOP Conference was held in New York on the subject of "Human Rights and the Liberation of Man in the Americas". Dom Helder Camara spoke; Reverend Wipfler was present, as were other Protestants and even members of the U.S. State Department. Attending the same conference was Mr. Thomas Quigley of the Latin American Department of the USCC, a co-worker with Father Colonnese. Quigley and Wipfler compared their information on repression in Brazil, and were determined to work together to make the public and the media aware of what was happening in Latin America.

Wipfler recounted that by 1969, his office was receiving daily reports of human rights violations in Latin America. He claimed that by that year he had received about 700 verifiable cases of torture in Brazil alone.[17] Efforts by the NCC to get the U.S. government to take notice and act on this information had been thwarted at every turn. In April of 1969, the Brazil Desk of the State Department went so far as to say that "There is very little that the U.S. can do and it is seeking to avoid any

_____

17
Interview with Reverend Wipfler, January 14, 1980.

conflict with the Roman Catholic activists". Catholic opposition to the Medici government was used as the official State Department excuse for not getting involved in the human rights problem in Brazil!

This was typical of the government attitude at the time. The Nixon Administration was more concerned with matters of international security and Viet Nam, rather than with either civil or international human rights. Needless to say, the Nixon-Kissinger national security mentality influenced the policy making of all quarters of the government. The State Department had refused to act, or even recognize reports of human rights violations in Brazil up to 1973. Rather it was official State Department policy to adhere to a strategy of "quiet diplomacy", the Nixon-Kissinger posture that informal, diplomatic discussion should be the only means by which human rights violations were to be addressed. No direct, open, action was to be taken which could conceivably be construed as American intervention in Latin American domestic affairs. Indeed, the Rockefeller Report and its findings which had been used to redesign U.S. Latin American relations, led to an increase in economic and military aid to Brazil and other countries, and stressed an attitude of equal partnership. The government believed that human rights complaints against Brazil in the 1969-1970 years would only harm

---

18
Unpublished minutes of a special Brazil meeting of the NCC.

the new U.S. foreign policy that the Nixon Administration had forged to deal with Latin America in the next decade.

The Congress, as well, was unconcerned about international human rights violations per se. In the late 1960's, the Viet Nam War had so pervaded the entire foreign policy decision making process that all other matters of international concern were given a lower priority.

Shortly after the CICOP conference in 1969, Wipfler was approached by some Brazilian students at Columbia University to put together a dossier of human rights violations in that country. Wipfler contacted Ralph Della Cava, a professor of history and a Brazil expert at Queens College; Brady Tyson, a former Protestant Missionary from Brazil who was a professor of Latin American Studies at American University in Washington; and Tom Quigley at the Latin American Division of the USCC. Together these men formed an organization known as the American Committee for Information on Brazil, prepared a dossier of human rights violations for public consumption, and collected signatures of persons concerned about the persecution in Brazil. They printed 1,000 copies of a dossier entitled "Terror in Brazil", and asked each recipient to send one dollar back to print other copies. Within months, they received ten thousand dollars; printed that many more copies, and began to create a constituency for concern about human rights violations in Brazil.

Further, they decided to meet on a regular basis and committed themselves to try to publicize the Brazilian cause in the media. Within the year, Della Cava wrote "Torture in Brazil", for Commonweal, Wipfler reported on "The Price of Progress in Brazil', for Christianity and Crisis, and Quigley placed articles in the Washington Post.

Thus, by the CICOP Conference of 1970, there was a growing American Catholic and Protestant concern for international human rights in Latin America. At that meeting, Colonnese, Wipfler and Quigley decided to put together an official dossier of human rights violations in Brazil from the files of the USCC and the NCC which could then be presented to an official international organization: the Inter-American Human Rights Commission of the Organization of American States. The idea was revolutionary: the two largest American Church institutions, former rivals, joining together in the name of morality to indict a foreign government for violating human rights.

While Quigley and Wipfler prepared the case, the USCC and the NCC continued to collect data and work closely on behalf of human rights matters. At the Latin American Division of the USCC, grass roots organizations were being formed to deal with human rights in Latin America; the Latin American Strategy Committee (an inter-denominational group) and CARRIBE (Committee Against Repression in Brazil), to augment the efforts of the American Friends of Brazil.

However, continued involvement in human rights by both the NCC and the USCC revealed clearly that repression in Brazil was not unique. Indeed, both organizations were receiving increased reports of violations from Argentina, Chile, Nicaragua and Uruguay. Other offices within their institutions were reporting similar incidents in other parts of the world as well, South Korea, the Philippines, Uganda, Burundi, Bangladesh and others. By 1977, both the USCC and the NCC were so inundated with information and pleas for help, that both had to reorganize and establish special offices for human rights within their agencies.

In 1970, however, neither the USCC nor the NCC were as knowledgeable, specialized or as politically astute as they are now. In fact, the first goal of both Quigley and Wipfler in bringing the case of Brazil to the OAS was to have an impact on the media. The fact that the OAS might investigate or call for sanctions against those who violated human rights in Brazil, or that such action might have political ramifications, was inconveivable to them at that time. Quigley referred to the action against Brazil as a "scattershot--a test".[19]

In May of 1970, the American Catholic Church, acting through the USCC, became the first U.S. religious denomination to denounce Brazil's human rights violations publicly. In a statement to the press, Father Colonnese, as head of the Latin American Division of the USCC stated:

19
Interview with Mr. Thomas Quigley, December 6, 1979.

On May 26, 1969, one year ago today, Father
Henrique Pereira Neto was brutally murdered
in Recife, Brazil his only crime being an
active concern for social justice and the
liberation of men.

No isolated instance, Father Pereira
Neto's death must be seen as part of a
wider picture of systematic terror. The
crippling of a Catholic student leader,
the imprisonment and beating of others,
including nuns and priests, the deportation
of North American and European missionaries,
the baseless accusations brought against
several Brazilian Bishops, even the attempted
suicide of a tortured Dominican friar--these
are 'instances' which add up to a campaign
of terror against the Catholic Church.

Nor is the church alone signaled out
for such treatment. Indeed even more
repressive measures are still accorded those
who do not have such ready access to world
public opinion as do leaders of Catholic
movements and members of the hierarchy....
WE DENOUNCE the reported campaign of widespread imprisonment, detention, threats,
harassments and even torture directed
against our fellow men and particulary our
fellow Catholics in Brazil;
WE CALL UPON the appropriate international
agencies, whether of the United Nations or
the Organization of American States, to
conduct a thorough on-site investigation
into the charges of systematic terror and
torture; and
WE URGE the immediate cessation of all U.S.
assistance, private as well as public, to
the government of Brazil should these
most grave allegations be substantiated. 20

20
    Press release of the USCC on May 26, 1970 entitled
"Statement on Brazil", pp. 1 and 2.

After the statement on Brazil, Father Colonnese, who claimed to speak for "the Catholic Church in the United States", called for direct action to supplement a "litany of interest" that could become a merely "meaningless ritual".[21] Colonnese outlined three measures that he believed would prove concern for international human rights. First, he called upon the Catholic press to "help form and inform U.S. Christian consciences".[22] Second, he urged the U.S. government to cease all aid to Brazil if the human right allegations against that country proved to be true.[23] Third, he encouraged the Vatican to break diplomatic relations with Brazil by calling home its Nuncio.[24]

The Catholic Church was now officially and actively involved in creating an American human rights movement, and from this point on, began to take more steps to educate and influence American society, the press, and the government in that regard. At the same time, the Church was also searching for ways to redress violations of human rights and to bring sanctions against those Latin American governments guilty of such repressive measures.

21
Statement of Father Louis Colonnese attached to the USCC "Statement on Brazil", May 26, 1970, pp. 2 and 3.

22
Ibid., p. 2.

23
Ibid., p. 3.

24
Ibid., p. 3.

The USCC Statement was soon followed by a similar one by the National Council of Churches in early June, 1970.

> ....Brazil has become a virtual police state,
> and accounts of the most brutal and humiliating
> tortures have been filtering out of the country
> since the fall of 1969. Allegations of political
> torture are not entirely new. Many Brazilians
> say that such torture began with the military
> take-over in 1964, although it was not until
> the fall of 1969 that these stories began to
> attract attention outside Brazil....
>   The Latin American Department, Division
> of Overseas Ministries of the National
> Council of Churches of Christ, U.S.A.
> declares its solidarity with the Committee
> of International Affairs of the U.S.
> Catholic Conference in its Brazil Statement....
>   We call upon the Congress of the United
> States to schedule a Congressional Hearing
> on the effects of the U.S. Government policy
> in Brazil, examining especially the nature
> and dimension of U.S. aid to determine to
> what extent public funds are used to support
> political repression in Brazil....
> We urge the Commission on Human Rights of
> the United Nations and the Commission on
> Human rights of the Organization of American
> States to initiate an investigation based on
> the numerous depositions and other evidence
> of torture in Brazil perpetrated upon
> students, professors, journalists, priests,
> nuns, ministers, politicians, lawyers,
> workers, artists and others. 25

The NCC, now, joined with its Catholic counterpart in a call for political action against Brazil. A new plateau had been reached. As the NCC and the USCC had become more involved, both organizations realized that they needed to influence not only the American public and press, but the government as well. And, as

---

25
    The National Council of Churches, "Statement on Political Repression and Terror in Brazil", June 5, 1970, pp. 1 and 2.

the NCC and the USCC continued to work together, their mutual interests helped to spawn other new ideas, create a sense of confidence to accomplish their goals, and strengthen their resolve to develop an American human rights constituency.

On June 25, 1970, their joint effort on behalf of human rights resulted in an indictment of Brazil before the OAS. On that day, information about repression in Brazil which had been gathered by the USCC and the NCC was presented to Dr. Gabino Fraga, the President of the Inter-American Commission on Human Rights of the OAS. Father Louis Colonnese made the presentation and requested "that the Inter-American Commission on Human Rights conduct a thorough on-site investigation of the charges of torture and repression in Brazil".[26] At the same time, a dossier of human rights violations was presented to the Pontifical Commission for Justice and Peace in Rome. Such an action had never been taken before, either by a government or a non-governmental organization although the potential to press for an investigation had existed for over twenty years.[27] Later, the

---

26
Letter of Rev. Louis Colonnese to Dr. Gabino Fraga, June 25, 1970.

27
Ian Brownlie, Basic Documents on Human Rights, (Oxford: Clarendon Press, 1971), pp. 414 and 415. See Chapter VII, Section 2, Article 4, of the American Convention on Human Rights. The Inter-American Commission on Human Rights came into existence in 1960 as an autonomous entity of the OAS. However, it was not until 1969 that the Statute establishing the function and powers of an Inter-American Court was signed.

efforts of the NCC and the USCC were augmented by support from Amnesty International and from the International Commission of Jurists as well.

The action of the USCC and the NCC served several purposes. First, it gave widespread American publicity to the repressive practices of the Brazilian government. When the case reached the media, it gave notice to the world that religious groups and other non-governmental organizations (NGO's), would band together to champion the cause of human rights around the globe to fight violations even if governments (as in the U.S.) would not be responsive to the plight of the abused. Second, it brought together voluntary organizations, from around the United States and other parts of the world, dealing with similar issues. A network of human rights organizations developed during the 1970's bringing together agencies involved in human rights, to exchange, classify, clarify, and use information to bring an awareness of repression to public view. Eventually, these organizations provided the information and credibility necessary to assist Congressonal endeavors to forge a foreign aid and assistance policy linked to human rights considerations.

The Brazil indictment, Case #1684, required three years to be heard and completed. The Inter-American Commission's work was a difficult task, particularly thwarted by the fact that the Brazilian government consistently refused to allow observers of international agencies such as the Red Cross or Amnesty

International to investigate the allegations of the USCC and the NCC. Also, the by-laws of the Commission required a constant update of human rights violations; thus both religious organizations had to continue to provide current information of repression in Brazil. That job fell to a Brazilian exile, one who had been imprisoned and was tortured himself, Marcos Santtamini de Arruda. However, after three years of documentation of human rights crimes by the workers of USCC, the NCC, and by Arruda, the OAS finally declared in 1974 at its Atlanta meeting that "evidence collected in this case leads to the persuasive presumption that in Brazil serious cases of torture, abuse and maltreatment have occurred to persons of both sexes while they were deprived of their liberty."[28]

It is difficult to assess the effect that Case #1684 had on the course of either U.S. or Brazilian human rights policy. On the surface, it appeared to be of little consequence. The OAS had asked the Brazilian government to carry out its own investigation of human rights violations by appointing independent judges to report back their findings to the Commission.[29] The Brazilian government never did this. The OAS also urged the Brazilian government "to punish, to the full

---

28
Organization of American States, Annual Report of the Inter-American Commission on Human Rights for the Year 1973, Fourth Regular Session, April 19, 1974, Atlanta, Georgia, p. 72.

29
Ibid., p. 73.

extent of the law, those persons that the evidence proves to have been responsible for violations of human rights".[30] The Brazilian government did not comply with this appeal. Nevertheless, the action taken by the USCC and the NCC against Brazil cannot be construed as a failure. For, this bold step encouraged other measures to be taken by both agencies to keep the human rights question before the eyes of the public. The USCC, in particular, began to enlarge the scope of its human rights concerns. In the early 1970's, that organization brought cases similar to Case #1684 before the OAS on behalf of those suffering persecution in Chile and Peru. Thomas Quigley, who had been working on Latin affairs exclusively for the USCC in the beginning of the decade noted that:

> Just a quick pass through the Chile files alone turns up over 20 cases for which case numbers [OAS case presentations] were assigned, some of these involving multiple affidavits, plus at least another six detailed submissions involving 254 persons in all.
> A few sample cases: #1769 Jentel, Casaldaliga et al (Brazil); #2030 Jose Arture Weibel (Chile); #2046 Dagoberto Perez Vargas (Chile); #2308 Jaime Troncose Valdes (Chile); #2572 Vladimir Herzog (Brazil); #3843 Cromotex Workers (Peru).[31]

Thus, in the early 1970's, the USCC was carrying out a very active schedule of case presentations to the OAS protesting human rights violations within Latin America. These cases often received attention in the media, particularly in the press, and it

---

30
   Ibid. p. 79
31
   Correspondence of Mr. Thomas Quigley to the author, October 28, 1980.

is possible to conclude that as a result of USCC action, a climate of American concern as well as a constituency for human rights evolved in the U.S. during the early 1970's.

At the same time, however, changes were occurring within the USCC which had a bearing on the later activities and scope of that agency. In 1971, Father Louis Colonnese, founder of CICOP and director of the Latin American Division of the USCC, was fired.

Called to the office of then Bishop Joseph Bernardin, the Director General of the USCC, Father Colonnese was told that his services were no longer required. Officially, the Bishop told Colonnese that there was a "lessening of confidence in his leadership", and that problems were occurring within his department because he "was unable to accept others opinions".[32] Colonnese responded publicly that "I have offended powerful men within the U.S. Church and they have fired me".[33] Privately, he believed that his ideas were too advanced for the USCC. Colonnese confided that his liberal Cuba stance seemed to him to be the real cause of his dismissal.[34] In 1971, then, the internal organization of the USCC underwent important changes. Father Fred Maquire, Father Colonnese's assistant, became the new

---

32
Statement of Bishop Joseph Bernadin, IDOC, North American Edition, October 30, 1971, p. 29.

33
Statement of Father Louis Colonnese, IDOC, North American Edition, October 30, 1971, p. 28.

34
Conversation with Father Colonnese, October 20, 1980.

Director of the Latin American Division of USCC, but since he was close to retirement, he only stayed on for two years. In 1973, Father J. Bryan Hehir, a Ph.D. in politics and ethics from Harvard, was recruited to direct a new office, that of International Justice and Peace. As a reorganization of the old office of International Affairs of the USCC, it incorporated the Latin American division formerly headed by Colonnese and Maguire. In that same year, CICOP died a quiet death after its last meeting in Dallas. Thus, 1973 marked the end of Father Colonnese's direct influence on the activities and policies of the USCC, the start of Father Hehir's administration, and a remarkable turn of events on Capitol Hill: the beginning of Congressional concern for international human rights.

III. Renewed U.S. Government Concern for Human Rights
    A. Congressional Impetus

After the USCC-NCC case against Brazil, articles about human rights violations around the world began to proliferate in the U.S. press. Disturbing news of massacres in Burundi and Bangladesh reached the headlines. The My Lai scandal, Vietnamese tiger cages, the insanity of Idi Amin, and the repression of Jews in the Soviet Union received wide media coverage. Similar stories about the Philippines and Greece, Brazil and Chile, and the wars in Northern Ireland and South Africa were in the forefront of the news daily.

In 1973, Representative Donald Fraser (D-Minn.), Chairman of the Subcommittee on International Movements and Organizations of

the House Committee on Foreign Affairs, decided to hold a series
of Congressional hearings on alleged human rights violations due
to mounting media, organizational and constituent pressures.[35]
"Concerned over rampant violations of human rights and the need
for a more effective response from both the U.S. and the world
community",[36] Fraser and his committee attempted to gain accurate
information about government persecution, repression, and abuses
around the globe. By utilizing selective case studies and
witnesses from government as well as international agencies and
non-governmental organizations (NGO's), the Fraser committee
jolted the Congress out of its complaceny about international
human rights beginning in 1973.

The USCC had an indirect, but positive influence on the call
for Congressional hearings by Fraser. The aim of the USCC
remember, during the late 1960's and early 1970's had been but
a limited one: to have an impact on the media and work with
other NGO's to create a climate and constituency concerned for
international human rights in the U.S. This goal apparently was
realized since Fraser did credit the media as being the factor
that most influenced him to call for human rights hearings in
1973.

---

[35] All information in reference to Representative Fraser's recollections on his first human rights hearings are the result of his correspondence with the author dated March 16, 1980.

[36] U.S., Congress, House, Subcommittee on International Movements and Organizations of the House Committee on Foreign Affairs, International Protection of Human Rights, 93rd. Cong., 1st. Sess., 1973, p. ix.

Fraser's perception of the role of the Catholic Church in assisting his committee after the hearings had begun is also important to this study. He believed that the religious groups did the most to help his committee. However, the only religious group present and testifying at the first series of hearings was the USCC and prominent members of the Catholic Church. Thus, it is possible to conclude that Fraser perceived the Catholic influence in relation to other NGO's as substantial, once the hearings had started. Fraser also felt that among the NGO's, the USCC had significant access to his committee. Indeed, if access to the government is to be equated with power, as some scholars contend,* then one must conclude that American Catholic influence on the Fraser committee was considerable as the hearings progressed. Due to the credible information that the USCC was able to supply to this commmittee, Catholic access grew since its reliability constituted one of the criteria by which individuals and groups were invited to testify. Among those Catholics included by Fraser in the first human rights hearings were John Cardinal Deardon, a representative of the National Council of Catholic Bishops and Archbishop of Detroit; members of the USCC, James Jennings and Thomas Quigley, and Father Theodore Hesburgh, President of the University of Notre Dame.

---

*
See David Truman, The Governmental Process, (New York: Alfred A. Knopf, 1965), Chapter 12.

Dr. John Salzberg, a specialist in human rights who had been hired by Congressman Fraser to put together the human rights hearings and who subsequently worked in the Office of Human Rights and Humanitarian Affairs at the State Department, believed that the Church witnesses helped the Fraser committee in a positive way. Often subjected to criticism by the press and conservative members of the Congress, the Fraser committee was placed in a defensive posture much of the time. Salzberg felt that the Church witnesses helped the image of the Committee, adding that the public perception of the Catholics was "good", that they provided reliable information, and that they were not vulnerable to the potential criticism of the other witnesses.[37]

Commenting on the start of the Fraser hearings, Salzberg noted that he had been in Washington only a few months, having been recruited a short time before to coordinate the activities of the committee. Therefore, he had to turn to the existing network of human rights NGO's for help to find witnesses, gain information, and get knowledgeable input for draft bills on legislation. One non-governmental organization, the Washington Office on Latin America,[*] suggested that Salzburg contact Thomas

---

[37]
Interview of the author with Dr. John Salzberg at the State Department, 18 February 1980.
[*]
Washington Office on Latin America (WOLA) is an inter-denominational organization which acts as a clearing house for information on Latin America and coordinates political activity to work for better U.S.-Latin American relations. USCC and the NCC are both participating members and often work in coalition with it on political problems of human rights in South America. It is headed by a returned Protestant missionary, Joseph Eldridge.

Quigley of the USCC for help. In August, Salzberg wrote to Quigley telling him of the impending hearings and requesting USCC input on several potential bills. At the same time, he invited Quigley to make recommendations for other legislation.[38]

The Fraser Committee, then, actively went out and sought the assistance of the USCC to help in its investigation of international human rights violations and to aid it in writing legislation to incorporate such principles into the practice of U.S. foreign policy. Salzberg felt that the Catholics had "more resources" to draw on than the other NGO's, especially information from missionaries, who could and did send reports about human rights conditions in the places where they were serving. Generally, however, Salzberg felt that Amnesty International had the largest NGO input, not the Catholic Church, whereas Fraser perceived the Church as playing a substantial role.

On the whole, however, the Fraser human rights hearings served to stimulate American Catholic involvement in the political process, particularly in the promotion of international human rights. Giving the USCC an entre into political circles, the hearings served to bring about better Church-State relations, and generally demonstrated that political activity by the Church was, indeed, acceptable and welcome to the government.

---

[38]
Unpublished correspondence of Salzberg to Quigley, August 9, 1973 and August 29, 1973.

The first Fraser hearings were not a comprehensive study of human rights violations around the globe, but they were exhaustive, and gave impetus to other hearings, and suggested twenty-nine recommendations for incorporating human rights into U.S. foreign policy.[39]   Seven significant pieces of legislation were initiated to that end.[40]

Further, they served to point out the differences in institutional thinking between the Executive and the Legislature. While the State Department, at the time, minimized human rights violations, and stressed instead the need for national security by a strategy of quiet diplomacy, the House chose to expose the

---

*
    Fraser held over 150 hearings on human rights between 1973 and 1978.

    39
    See the report of the Fraser hearings: U.S., Congress, House, Subcommittee on International Organizations and Movements, Human Rights in the World Community, A Case of U.S. Leadership, 93rd. Cong., 2nd. Sess., 1974.   For an assessment see: John Salzberg and Donald D. Young, "The Parliamentary Role in Implementing International Human Rights: A. U.S. Example", Texas International Law Journal, 12 (25:1977): 251-278.

    40
    See House Resolution 556, September 20, 1973 (Better use of the International Court of Justice at the Hague); House Resolution 557, September 20, 1973 (To ratify the U.N. Covenants on Human Rights); House Concurrent Resolution 307, September 20, 1973 (To promote humane rules of war); House Concurrent Resolution 310, September 20, 1973 (To strengthen the U.N. Human Rights Commission); House Concurrent Resolution 321, September 20, 1973 (To establish rules for the treatment of prisoners); House Concurrent Resolution 313, September 20, 1973 (To support U.N. efforts to establish a program for the decade to combat racism and racial discrimination); and House Resolution 10455, September 20, 1973 (To establish an office within the State Department on Humanitarian Affairs).

repression in Latin America, Asia and other parts of the world. Furthermore, Congress emphasized the American responsibility to support international human rights openly by eventually making it a criteria for the reception of U.S. foreign aid. At the same time, the Fraser hearings also helped to stimulate other Congressional activity on behalf of international human rights and rallied a constituency of such legislators as Senators Humphrey, McGovern, Abourezk, Cranston, Kennedy, Church and Jackson; and Representatives Harkin, Fenwick, Fascell, Badillo, Dellums and Abzug.

The Foreign Assistance Act of 1973 best reflected the changing mood of the Congress toward human rights. Translating that attitude into legislation, Senator James Abourezk (D-S.D.) introduced a bill which called for new directions in developmental aid based on human need. Essentially, his bill expressed the sense of Congress that the President should deny economic and/or military assistance to countries which persecuted their citizens for political activity, and that U.S. funds to support police training abroad should be prohibited. Concommitantly, Senator Edward Kennedy (D-Mass.) introduced a new section to the Foreign Assistance Act which stated that human rights should be protected in Chile.[41] Thus, with the passage of

---

[41]
See Public Law 93-189, December 17, 1973, Sections 32, 112 and 35, in 22 USC 2151, Sec. 35 and 22 USC 2151 Sec. 32 and 22 USC 2151, Sec. 112.

Abourezk's and Kennedy's bills as part of the Foreign Assistance Act, 1973 became a landmark for U.S. Congressional activity on behalf of international human rights. The Fraser Committee and the Congressional concern for human rights, evidenced in hearings and legislation within that year, were forecasts of a renewed interest in the need to protect the fundamental freedom of all men.

In 1974, the now famous Section 502B of the Foreign Assistance Act was enacted by the Congress. The strongest U.S. statement up to that time on human rights, it called for action, not simply diplomatic discussion, when dealing with those nations that consistently violated human rights. It stated that it was:

> the sense of Congress, that in extraordinary
> circumstances, the President shall substan-
> tially reduce or terminate security assis-
> tance to any government which engages in a
> consistent pattern of gross violations of
> internationally recognized human rights,
> including torture or cruel, or inhuman or
> degrading treatment or punishment, pro-
> longed detention without charges; or other
> flagrant denials of the right to life,
> liberty and the security of the person. 42

Further, the Foreign Assistance Act of 1974 cut off military aid to Chile and limited economic assistance to that country. It also stipulated that if the President continued military aid despite the abuses of human rights in a country, he would have to

---

42
    Section 502B of the Foreign Assistance Act of 1974,
88 <u>Stat</u>. 1815 (1974)

justify such action to the Congress. Curbing military assistance to South Korea unless that country made substantial progress in human rights, the Act also prohibited funds for the training of police and security agents.[43]

In that same year, Senator Henry Jackson of Washington attempted to tie trade to respect for human rights.[44] Attempting to enact legislation which would link Soviet emigration policies to U.S. preferential trade treatment, it was his aim to make respect for human rights a component of detente. Thus, concern for international human rights now began to include trade as well as aid, and east-west interests as well as north-south ones.

By 1974, then, the Congress had made known its desire that the President connect the humane treatment of individuals to U.S. foreign policy decisions. However, since the Nixon Administration continued to pursue its policy of "quiet diplomacy" and was so mired in Watergate, the White House gave restricted Executive support to the matter of international human rights. On November 14, 1975, the State Department sent a report to the Congress on the matter of security assistance and human rights. It stated rather plainly:

43
Public Law 93-559, December 30, 1974.

44
See Title IV of the Trade Act of 1974.

In view of the widespread nature of human
rights violations in the world, we have
found no adequately objective way to make
distinctions of degree between nations.
This fact leads us, therefore, to the
conclusion that neither the U.S. security
interest nor the human rights cause would
be properly served by the public obliquy
and impaired relations with security
assistance recipient countries that would
follow the making of inherently subective
U.S. government determinations that 'gross
violations' do or do not exist or that a
'consistent pattern' of such violation does
or does not exist in such countries. 45

Essentially then, the Nixon Administration, through the

State Department, minimized human rights considerations in the

granting of security assistance as late as 1975. Congress, on

the other hand, refused to be cowed by the Nixon policy of "quiet

diplomacy" or by the rhetoric of the State Department. In 1975,

Congressman Thomas Harkin (D-Iowa) introduced a bill to amend the

Foreign Assistance Act, (Public Law 94-302), Section 116 of his

bill changed the "sense of Congress" suggestion to limit security

aid to nations that violated human rights, by specifically

prohibiting any U.S. development aid to such nations, "unless

such assistance would directly benefit the needy people in such

country". Further, Harkin's legislation empowered either the

45
Report of the State Department to the Congress on the human
rights situation in countries receiving U.S. security assistance.
Quoted in U.S., Congress, House, Human Rights and U.S. Foreign
Assistance., 96th Cong., 1st Sess., 1979, p. 18.

46
Public Law 94-302, May 31, 1976, Sections 28 and 211.

House International Relations Committee or the Senate Foreign Relations Committee to require a written report demonstrating how the aid would help those in need in other nations. Provisions authorizing the House or the Senate to initiate action to terminate development assistance if they disagreed with the President were included. Harkin's bill further required the President to submit annual reports to the Congress proving compliance with these provisions while stipulating that cooperation with international agencies investigating human rights violations would play a part in determining whether or not nations were truly sincere about the protection of human rights.

In 1976, Congress continued to tighten restrictions on aid to nations which violated human rights. Again authoring such legislation, Congressman Harkin sponsored a bill requiring the Executive Directors of the Inter-American Development Bank and the African Development Fund to vote against any loan or financial or technical assistance to any nations that "engaged in a consistent pattern of gross violations of internationally recognized human rights".[47] In the same year, as part of the International Security and Arms Export Control Act, Congress finally enacted legislation suggested by the Fraser hearings in 1973: it officially established a Coordinator for Human Rights

---

[47]
International Development and Food Assistance Act of 1975, 89 Stat. 849 (codified in scattered sections of Titles 7,12 and 22 USC).

and Humanitarian Affairs within the State Department to be appointed by the President.[48] More importantly, it required the Secretary of State to submit yearly reports to the Congress on human rights practices in those countries receiving security assistance, and the steps taken by the U.S. government to promote human rights in those countries. If those reports were not forthcoming, Congress could interrupt aid; and if the reports showed human rights violations, Congress could terminate aid by a joint resolution.[49]

---

[48]
Public Law 94-329, June 30, 1976. In April of 1975, Deputy Secretary of State Robert Ingersoll appointed James Wilson to comply with requests from the Congress for someone to handle the growing human rights concerns of that branch of the government. Wilson was to centralize and handle matters of refugees, humanitarian assistance, problems of prisoners of war and work with the Red Cross and other voluntary rights agencies. Later, the office was elevated to the Assistant Secretary rank by Public Law 95-105, and became a bureau within the State Department. It had three divisions: the Office of Human Rights, the Office of Refugees and Migration Affairs, and the Office of Prisoners of War and Missing in Action. In 1977, President Carter appointed Ms. Patricia Derian, a civil rights worker in the past, as first head of that Bureau.

[49]
The original version allowed Congress to terminate aid by a concurrent resolution that is, without the consent of the President. This was vetoed by President Ford on May 7, 1976, who believed that the bill encroached on his powers in foreign affairs. It was sent back to the House, where is was agreed that a joint resolution would be used instead to terminate aid. The latter type of resolution requires agreement between the Congress and the President and requires the Executive signature to implement the termination of aid.

In 1977, revisions of two significant pieces of legislation were enacted to strengthen U.S. human rights policies. First, the International Development and Food Assistance Act of 1977 brought changes to Section 116D of the Foreign Assistance Act. Having previously required that yearly status reports be published by the State Department on countries receiving U.S. development assistance, the new law mandated that the Agency for International Development (AID) now had to do the same. Further, $750,000 was designated for programs to encourage international human rights, and Section 112 was added to Title I of the Agricultural Trade Development and Assistance Act of 1954 prohibiting the sale of agricultural products to nations violating human rights unless it directly benefited needy people.[50] Second, the Omnibus Multilateral Development Institutions Act of 1977 (H 52262) authorized and instructed the U.S. Executive Directors of all international financial institutions (IFI's) to vote against loans, and financial or technical assistance to countries that violated human rights, unless it was shown to serve the basic human needs of the people. It also required the government to initiate meetings with other nations to develop standards and mechanisms to meet basic human needs and to protect human rights.[51]

---

[50] Public Law 95-88, August 3, 1977.

[51] Public Law 95-118, October 3, 1977.

In 1978, the Congress moved to mandate other agencies of the government to incorporate human rights considerations into the practice of their international dealings. The overseas Private Investment Corporation (OPIC) Amendments Act of 1978 encouraged respect for human rights. It allowed investments by that agency only where human rights were observed, and under other conditions only if it benefited the needy or met national security requirements. In the same year, the President was authorized 1.5 million dollars for development assistance funds to promote programs to encourage international human rights by the International Development and Food Assistance Act.[52] At the same time, the Foreign Relations Authorization Act expressed the sense of Congress that freedom of information should be encouraged around the globe.[53] Of most significance that year was the revision of Section 502B of the Foreign Assistance Act, as amended in the International Security Act of 1978. Now, what had simply been a statement of support for human rights previously was backed by the requirement, as stipulated in 502B, that security assistance be denied to any government engaged in gross violations of international human rights. It also prohibited security assistance to the police and internal intelligence agencies of such countries, and disallowed the sale of

---

[52]
Public Law 95-424, October 10, 1978.

[53]
Public Law 95-426, October 7, 1978.

instruments of crime control to them as well. In that same year, the International Monetary Fund Supplementary Financing Facility also required the Secretary of the Treasury to meet with the Secretary of State and submit to the Congress a yearly report on international human rights practices in countries using its services.[55]

Thus, in the five years between 1973 and 1978, the Congress developed a core of legislation which not only established a concern for international human rights, but which placed restrictions and sanctions on those nations which violated them. The legislation was a natural outgrowth of Congressional hearings on human rights held within the same time frame. The Fraser Committee called individual sessions to investigate human rights violations in Haiti, Chile, the Soviet Union, Indonesia, the Philippines, Iran, Nicaragua, Guatemala, El Salvador, India, Uruguay, Paraguay, Argentina, North Korea, East Timor, Cambodia, Taiwan, Thailand, Vietnam, South Korea and Brazil. The combined Congressional activity on behalf of human rights, the hearings which kept the issue in the news and developed a legislative constituency, and the passage of human rights legislation, helped to involve other government agencies as well as the Executive in the cause of international human rights. Religious groups and other NGO's played a part in helping to influence the Congress in

---

54
  Public Law 95-384, September 26, 1978.

55
  Public Law 95-435, October 10, 1978.

revealing and redressing the human rights violations around the globe. They supplied objective information when the State Department would or could not. They created an initial awareness of human rights violations by their impact on the media and actions before the OAS. Their influence was indirect, but positive nonetheless.

B. Executive Policy

Congressional activity during the 1973-1975 period on behalf of international human rights was carried out with limited executive support from President Nixon, President Ford and the Secretary of State, Henry Kissinger. Gerald Ford continued the Nixon-Kissinger policy of "quiet diplomacy" until 1975, but did allow the U.S. to become party to the Helsinki Accords, an international step toward advancing global human rights.

The Helsinki Accords were a result of the Conference on Security and Cooperation in East Europe which had been called by the Soviet Union in 1973. The purpose of the Conference, to legitimatize the borders of Eastern Europe by treaty, ended with surprising results. While the participating states agreed to accept the East European borders by declaration, the Western allies succeeded in negotiating an accord* which reflected international human rights concerns.

The Helsinki Final Act contained three sections or "baskets", the third of which essentially called for adherence to

_____
* An accord is a declaration of intentions, but does not have the binding force of a treaty.

the principles of the U.N. Universal Declaration of Human Rights. Enumerating these fundamental rights, the Helsinki Final Act became not only a modern day reassertion of international human rights, but for the first time, officially tied such considerations to American-Soviet detente. Thus, President Gerald Ford in 1975, took the first Executive action to reconcile concern for international human rights with foreign policy. In 1975, then, a slight shift in executive strategy occurred: a move from total national security priorities in foreign policy to the gradual injection of human rights concerns into such decision making processes.

In 1976 the new President, Jimmy Carter, grasped the momentum of the situation, campaigned for human rights, and announced at his inauguration that human rights would be the criterion for his foreign policy endeavors. On taking office he said:

> Because we are free, we can never be indifferent
> to the fate of freedom elsewhere. Our moral
> sense dictates a clear preference for those
> societies which share with us an abiding respect
> for individual human rights. 56

Soon after being sworn in, the President filled the post of Coordinator for Humanitarian Affairs and Human Rights with the appointment of Ms. Patricia Derian, a long time civil rights

---

56
President Jimmy Carter, "the Inaugural Address of President Jimmy Carter", Department of State Bulletin, 76 (February 14, 1977): 122

activist.   The   subsequent appointment of Mark Schneider as   her

assistant, as well as the appointment of Cyrus Vance as Secretary

of State and Warren Christopher as Deputy Secretary of State were

further   evidence   of the priority that human rights   would   have

during the Carter Presidency.   These people were deeply committed

to   the   principle of human rights in foreign policy   and   worked

toward that end during their government service.

In March 1977, Christopher unveiled the new State Department

attitude toward human rights.   He said:

> The concern for human rights will be woven
> into the fabric of our foreign policy.   If
> we are to do justice to our goals, we must
> act always with a concern to achieve practical
> results and with an awareness of the other
> demands on our diplomacy.   When it is desirable
> to do so, we will speak out, trying to be neither
> strident nor polemical....We may decide to com-
> municate by quiet diplomacy with the country
> involved to see what can be accomplished that
> way.   Or we may prefer to approach the problem
> not bilaterally, but through multilateral
> channels.   In some instances of human rights
> violations, assistance programs may be curtailed,
> but we must also recognize that to be evenhanded,
> we should not just penalize but also inspire,
> persuade, and reward....There should be no
> mistake: The undertaking to promote human rights
> is now an integral part of our foreign policy....
> We are working to fulfill both the letter and the
> spirit of current legislation relating human
> rights concerns to foreign assistance. 58

57
   Warren Christopher,   "Human Rights: An Important Concern of
U.S. Foreign Policy", Department of State Bulletin, 76 (March 28,
1977): 289-290.

By May of 1977, Secretary of State Vance attempted to define the executive understanding of human rights, and to explain the U.S. commitment to such concerns in foreign policy. At Law Day ceremonies at the University of Georgia School of Law, he defined human rights:

> First, there is the right to be free from
> governmental violation of the integrity of
> the person. Such violations include torture;
> cruel, inhuman or degrading treatment or
> punishment; and arbitrary arrest or imprison-
> ment. And they include denial of fair public
> trial and invasion of the home. Second, there
> is the right to the fulfillment of such vital
> needs as food, shelter, health care, and
> education. We recognize that the fulfillment
> of this right will depend, in part, upon the
> stage of a nation's economic development. But
> we also know that this right can be violated
> by a government's action or inaction--for
> example, through corrupt official processes
> which divert resources to an elite at the
> expense of the needy or through indifference
> to the plight of the poor. Third, there is
> the right to enjoy the civil and political
> liberties: freedom of thought, of religion,
> of assembly; freedom of speech; freedom of
> the press; freedom of movement both within
> the outside one's own country; freedom to
> take part in government.
> Our policy is to promote all these rights....
> If we are determined to act, the means avail-
> able range from quiet diplomacy in its many
> forms, through public pronouncements, to
> withholding of assistance. Whenever possible,
> we will use positive steps of encouragement
> and inducement. Our strong support will go
> to countries that are working to improve the
> human condition. We will always try to act
> in concert with other countries, through
> international bodies....This Administration's
> human rights policy has been framed in
> collaboration and consultation with Congress
> and private organizations. We have taken

steps to assure firsthand contact, consultation, and observation when members of Congress
travel abroad to review human rights conditions. 58

The Secretary's open reference to NGO input into the
formulation of U.S. human rights foreign policy is most
interesting in this study. For it shows, rather conclusively,
that the work of the USCC, and many other human rights groups did
have a positive effect on the executive as well as the
legislative branch of the government.

The first two years of the Presidency of Jimmy Carter might
well be characterized as the Golden Age of Human Rights Foreign
Policy for the United States. The body of legislation passed by
the Congress from 1973 on, was finally given Presidential support
and supplemented by executive action to reflect human rights as a
significant priority in American foreign policy. Early in 1977,
the State Department backed a U.N. measure decrying the taking of
hostages and called for the cessation of U.S. purchases of
Rhodesian chrome by urging the repeal of the Byrd Amendment.
Supporting the British in their call for a U.N. investigation
into the death of Ugandan Archbishop Janani Luwum, the State
Department furthered the executive commitment to human rights.
The President, himself, had openly corresponded with Andrei
Sakharov after the State Department protested the treatment of

---

58
    Secretary of State Cyrus Vance, "Human Rights and Foreign
Policy", Department of State Bulletin, 76
(May 23, 1977) :505-507.

Czech members of Charter 77. And. within three months of taking office, the new President appeared at the U.N. and expounded the basic priorities of U.S. foreign policy: peace, arms control, economic progress and human rights.[59] To show his good faith a few months later, the President signed two significant U.N. Covenants that had never received presidential approval: the Covenant on Economic, Social and Cultural Rights and the Covenant on Civil and Political Rights (treaty forms of the Universal Declaration of Human Rights). Carter further recommended the confirmation of the Genocide Convention which had been signed, but not approved by the Senate. Later, in June, the President continued his activity on behalf of human rights by signing the American Convention on Human Rights of the OAS Charter, dormant since 1948.

---

*

    This was an organization established in Czechoslovakia to monitor government compliance with the Helsinki Final Act. It was composed of Czech writers, scientists, and other members of the society, later branded as "dissidents" by the government. Its parallel organization in the Soviet Union was the Helsinki Watch Movement founded by Uri Orlov and other "dissidents".

59
    President Jimmy Carter, "Remarks on Signing [the] International Covenants on Human Rights", "Weekly Compilation of Presidential Documents", Vol. 13, No. 18 (October 5, 1977), pp. 1488-1489.

As the first year of President Carter's administration drew to a close, a new sense of foreign policy priorities was evident. Presidential speeches during the year and State Department cooperation with the Congress to promote human rights were changing the course of American international affairs. In December of 1977, the State Department issued statements supporting the release of the Myongdong prisoners in Korea, 11,000 detainees in Pakistan, and 935 incarcerated people in Bangladesh. In February 1978, as the President took his first trip abroad, he felt so comfortable with the new human rights factor in American foreign policy that he felt free to speak out for fundamental freedoms when he visited Poland, South East Asia and the Middle East.

In July 1978, the State Department again spoke out on international repression. It condemned Cambodia for genocide, and a few months later, openly expressed its concern for the trials of two Soviet dissidents, Alexander Scharansky and Alexander Ginzberg.

This governmental turn about was reflected in the Belgrade Conference held in 1977 and 1978 as a follow-up to find ways to implement the provisions of the Final Act of the Helsinki Accords. However, during the two intervening years, between the meetings at Helsinki and Belgrade, Charter 77 and the Helsinki Soviet Watch Movement were organized by private citizens behind the Iron Curtain to monitor Soviet compliance with the provisions of the Final Act. In the United States, a Congressional human rights watchdog committee was also established by the efforts of Millicent Fenwick (R-N.J.), known as the U.S. Committee on Security and Cooperation in Europe. Thus, by the Belgrade meeting in 1977-8, human rights was gaining an international constituency supported by the U.S. and "dissidents" abroad.

The U.S. representative to the Belgrade Conference was Arthur Goldberg, former Supreme Court Justice and Ambassador to the United Nations. While much of the meeting revolved around Soviet human rights violations and Communist counter charges against the United States, nevertheless, for the first time since World War II, human rights was the most significant matter to be considered at an internationnal forum.

The Carter Administration continued its pursuit of human rights through 1978 and 1979, scoring Latin American countries for their repression as well as the Soviet Union, other Communist nations, Asian states and African countries.

In April of 1979, the U.S. committment to human rights seemed to reach its peak when the American government exchanged two convicted Soviet spies to secure the freedom of five Russian "dissidents": Eduard Kuznetsov, Georgi Vins, Mark Dymshits, Valentin Moroz and Alexander Ginzburg.

However, the hostage crisis in November 1979, and the Mid-East War between Iran and Iraq in 1980, changed the focus of the Carter foreign policy. Forced into a more "pragmatic", and "realistic", approach to international affairs, the President had to give national security and defense needs a higher priority in U.S. foreign policy. His repudiation by the American public at the polls in the election of the fall of 1980, signaled the demise of a foreign policy based mainly on a forthright respect for human rights.

IV. Conclusion

The years 1965-1978 saw human rights re-emerge as a significant international concern of both the American Catholic Church and the U.S. government. The Church's interest in human rights was renewed by its desire to help its persecuted brothers in Latin America. After a period of complacency during the Cold War years, the government's involvement on behalf of human rights developed during the late 1960's and 1970's as a result of the Fraser hearings and Congressional legislation to tie foreign aid and trade to respect for fundamental rights.

The American Catholic Church, particularly through the United States Catholic Conference, took measures in the mid-1960's to publicize repression in Brazil, to create a climate of concern for international human rights generally, and to develop an American constituency interested in the problem of religious and political repression around the world. It did this first by simple programs of advocacy, then by working with other religious groups, particularly the NCC, to publish information about terror in Latin America. In 1970, the United States Catholic Conference and the National Council of Churches took their human rights concerns one step farther to the OAS and sought sanctions against Brazil for violations of human rights. This was the beginning of Catholic and Protestant attempts not only to publicize, but to bring sanctions against governments that engaged in repression. By 1973, the American Catholic Church became politically involved on behalf of international human rights. Invited to testify at the Fraser hearings, the USCC began to participate in the political arena to insure the fact that human rights became a factor in U.S. foreign policy.

The U.S. government manifested its concern for human rights in 1973, when Congressman Donald Fraser called the first official government hearings to consider human rights violations and their implication for U.S. foreign policy. As a result of Fraser's hearings between 1973 and 1978, human rights became a subject of intense Congressional study, and a factor in the granting of U.S. foreign aid. A body of human rights legislation was passed by the Congress between 1973 and 1978 and, concomitantly, the executive also began to shift from a posture of "quiet diplomacy" to a foreign policy formulated with the human rights factor as a prime consideration.

Although there does not appear to be any direct link between the early activities of the American Catholic Church on behalf of international human rights, and the initial concern of the government as shown in the Fraser hearings, there was an indirect link through the media. The Church's impact on the press served to heighten Congressional awareness of repression as Congressman Fraser stated. It kept the issue of human rights before the public and the government until some action was finally taken by the Congress to address the problem. Moreover, as the Church assisted the Fraser Committee substantially in the course of its human rights investigations over the years, Church influence on the Congress became more positive. And, as we shall see in the next Chapter, Church efforts to lobby for specific pieces of human rights legislation also had an impact on the Congress and the devleopment of a more moral foreign policy during the decade as well.

CHAPTER V: FUNCTIONS AND PROBLEMS OF THE AMERICAN
CHURCH IN WORKING FOR THE DEVELOPMENT OF
A U.S. HUMAN RIGHTS POLICY

I. Introduction

This chapter will ask two questions. First, what are the
functions of the American Catholic Church in its endeavors to
promote international human rights?   Second, what problems
existed which compromised the effectiveness of the Church in its
efforts on behalf of human rights up to the 1980's?   With regard
to the first question, the American Catholic Church carries out
its work in the area of human rights through the National
Conference of Catholic Bishops (NCCB), and its advisory adjunct,
the United States Catholic Conference (USCC). Working in tandem,
these organizations carry out three functions designed to promote
international human rights: monitoring and/or classifying data,
educating and/or publishing information, and lobbying.   These
activities were carried out in a limited way, however, up to the
1980's, due to a number of factors which mitigated against the
Church's ability to be more effective in its efforts on behalf of
human rights.   The primary reasons for this were the Church's
commitment to a diverse number of issues, its lack of hierarchial
support for human rights, its unique international position, and
the uncertainty among its leaders as to what political role, if
any, the Church should play to promote human rights.   These
problems were resolved, however, during the 1980's and their
effects will be addressed later.

II. The Functions of the Church in its Work for Human Rights
     A. General Organizational Structure

As a result of Vatican II, both the authority and the duties of the world's Catholic Bishops were redefined in light of the current social and Catholic institutional needs. The Council, in Christus Dominus, stressed the collegial nature of the episcopate, encouraged the development of regional, hierarchical organizations, and emphasized the importance of the role of the Bishops to work for the improvement of the social, as well as the spiritual, well-being of their flocks. In the United States, the old National Catholic Welfare Conference (NCWC), which had been in existence under various names since the end of World War I, was reorganized in 1966 to meet the new focus of Catholic concerns. The National Conference of Catholic Bishops (NCCB) was established at that time in response to the mandate of Vatican II for a collegial, regional, episcopate. As a canonical organization, the NCCB acts as a voluntary, collective agency in pastoral matters, and makes policy on issues of significant religious and social import.

In 1966 the United States Catholic Conference was also set up to assist the American Bishops in carrying out their societal responsibilities. As a reorganization of the old NWCW, the USCC was established as a civil corporation based on committees of lay people, clergy and religious, headed by Bishops. It advises, reviews, and implements policies of the Bishops Conference, but has no policy making authority of its own. However, due to the day to day nature of its work, the USCC makes daily decisions, which in effect, become part of Catholic policy in the economic, educational, social and political spheres.

The specific matter of human rights, and work related to it, falls within the jurisdiction of the Office of International Justice and Peace (OIJP) of the USCC.* Broadly, the OIJP handles matters that pertain to international relations. It advises the American Bishops on foreign policy and implements their policies through the media and participation in the political arena.

During the crucial decade of the 1970's, the director of the OIJP was Father J. Bryan Hehir, a young, dynamic priest dedicated to social justice. With a Ph.D. in politics and ethics from Harvard, Hehir presides over a small, but able staff. The OIJP specialist on human rights at the time was Mrs. Patricia Rengle, a graduate of Georgetown University Law School with a concentration of study in law and social policy. Her desk became a separate area of specialization within the OIJP during the decade. Mr. Thomas Quigley, from the University of Michigan, and

---

*

OIJP was actually founded in 1973 after several reorganizations of the USCC. It combined the Office of International Affairs and the desks of other individual countries into one department in that year.

who was instrumental in bringing the first joint Catholic-Protestant human rights case against Brazil at the OAS, is still involved in working for human rights within the OIJP. His area of expertise is actually Latin America. Other members of OIJP include individuals who deal with political trends and ecclesiastical relationships in the Third World; political/military affairs, South American documentation and African affairs. There is a support staff of five persons, including secretaries and librarians.

OIJP gathers information on international matters which are of concern to the Bishops, keeps the Bishops advised as to current economic, political and military trends, and essentially carries out the foreign policy of the Catholic Church in America. Because it is not possible for the OIJP to check with the Bishops on each and every matter of international import, it must make decisions based on a policy of Catholic tradition, Papal statements and encyclicals, and American pastoral letters; in short, from a "patchwork" magisterium. Although the OIJP cannot make policy directly, the strategies which it recommends are often the accepted stances of the American hierarchy, and the activities which it carries out within the confines of episcopal limits help to shape the speed and direction with which certain policies are implemented. Thus, it is possible to conclude that the OIJP is a formidable voice in the development of Catholic international concerns.

On the particular issue of human rights, the OIJP works to obtain information from abroad that might be of use to the U.S. Bishops in their formulation of an American Catholic response to repression. Such information is also used as the basis for Catholic testimony to the Congress. OIJP works to publicize the abuse of human rights around the world and, tries to influence the government to incorporate human rights into the foreign policy decision making process.

B. The Monitoring Function

Gathering information about human rights violations has been one of the most important tasks of OIJP since its inception. Samples of correspondence attest to a continuous flow of such information from Latin America to that office. An unpublished letter from Father Hehir to former Secretary of State Cyrus Vance indicates this. Hehir wrote: "...Hardly a week goes by that our office does not receive information on new arrests or disappearances..."[1] In 1978, the Argentine reports of human rights violations became so heavy that an unpublished office memo from Thomas Quigley to Father Hehir showed the difficulty OIJP had in keeping up with the pleas for help:

---

[1] Unpublished letter of Father Hehir to Secretary Cyrus Vance, November 18, 1977.

> For almost two years, we have been receiving
> urgent appeals for us to do something regard-
> ing issues in Argentina. Hardly a week goes
> by that we do not receive new information,
> cases, requests, etc....I believe we should
> institute a more routine system of communicat-
> ing our concerns, sending such major requests
> as we receive on to the Argentine Conference. 2

Correspondence arrives in large quantities from hierarchy, clergy, and missionaries about human rights violations occurring around the globe. Supplemented with mail from lay individuals, these letters, as well as affidavits and pictures, are categorized and kept on file to substantiate Catholic protests about human rights violations made to members of international agencies, embassies, or U.S. government bodies.

Such data is used only in a general way as the basis for the reliable testimony. Both Congressman Fraser and Dr. Salzberg commended the USCC and depended on that data upon for their series of over 150 human rights hearings from 1973 to 1978. No information, however, is ever used that would compromise the safety of particular individuals, the clergy, or the Church in the specific country where repression is reported.

In the case of Brazil, data on human rights violations has been catalogued in a three inch thick dossier which is kept in the offices of OIJP. Pictures and sworn statements of hundreds of victims of repression, as well as the countless letters from

---

2
Unpublished memo of Thomas Quigley to Father Hehir, April 18, 1978. The Argentine Conference referred to here is the episcopal organization of the Argentine hierarchy.

parents and friends of murdered political casualties can be read there.   The Reverend Wipfler also has a comparable dossier, kept under security, at the National Council of Churches documenting human rights abuses in Chile.   Wipfler commented that if ever a trial for human rights violators were to be held indicting Brazilian or Chilian officials such as the one held at Nuremburg, both the USCC and the NCC would be prepared to present evidence against the perpetrators.[3]

OIJP also gathers information from ex-prisoners and victims of persecution (both clerical and lay) who happen, for some reason, to be in the United States and wish to tell of their experiences. Again, such facts are used only in a general way to protect the individuals and the Church from retaliation.   For example, the OIJP had been receiving information about the tyrannical tactics of the Amin government in Uganda during the early 1970's.   But, the Catholic Ugandan hierarchy had requested that the OIJP not make any statements opposing the regime, fearing that overt criticism might trigger reprisals against the clergy or members of the Catholic Church in Uganda.   The OIJP

3
Interview with the Reverend Wipfler, January 14, 1980.

4
Interview with Thomas Quigley, December 6, 1979.

never openly criticized the Amin regime. After the British government had attacked Amin's policies, and the questionable death of Archbishop Janai Luwum, an Anglican prelate in Uganda occurred, OIJP silence seemed justified. Thus, oftentimes when the Church is criticized for its lack of open criticism, there are usually extentuating circumstances which dictate such a course of action. The OIJP is extremely cautious in the use and referral of its information.

Data, again in a general way, is exchanged by the OIJP with other non-governmental organizations working in the area of human rights. A large network presently exists in the U.S. and abroad to monitor human rights. The most well known of these agencies are Amnesty International, the International Commission of Jurists, and the International Red Cross. The OIPJ interacts with all these, as well as with many more national organizations which also gather information, pass it along the U.S. human rights network and labor for a more humane international affairs. Among these smaller groups, the OIJP works in concert with The Friends Committee, Christians Concerned for Chile, the Chile Committee for Human Rights, the Office for Political Prisoners and Human Rights in Chile, the Chile Solidarity Committee, the U.S. Committee for Justice to Latin American Political Prisoners, the Interreligious Task Force on U.S. Food Policy, the Center for International Policy, the Jesuit Project on Third World

Awareness, the Coalition for a New Foreign and Military Policy (as part of its Human Rights Working Group), the Washington Office on Latin America, the Naitonal Council of Churches, and many others sponsored by religious orders.

C. The Educational Function

The second important task of OIJP in the area of human rights is the educational one. Its purpose is to teach and inform the general public, and Catholics in particular, the media, and the government about international human rights in an attempt to create a constituency for such concerns.

Public awareness of human rights is promoted by OIJP publications, news releases, interviews and briefings. Current publications include "Human Rights--Human Needs", "Human Rights Reflections on a Twin Anniversary", "U.S. Foreign Policy: A Critique from Catholic Tradition", "Arms Export Policies-- Ethical Choices", and "Human Rights--A Priority for Peace".[5]

Interviews and briefings are techniques seldom used by the OIJP. These activities are carried out sparingly and only used to underscore important actions taken by that office. For example, in 1970 officials of the USCC and the NCC held a joint press conference in Washington to protest human rights violations and Church persecution by the military government of Brazil. Open letters to individuals seems to be used more often to inform

---

5
    These pamphlets are all available through the USCC bookstore which also answers mail requests.

important persons about events that are occurring which relate to international human rights. For example, in 1971 when General Medici, the President of Brazil, was visiting the U.S., an open letter was sent by the OIJP to members of the government and the press to urge the end of repression in his country. Other uses of the open letter are documented in OIJP files.

The OIJP educates Catholics about human rights by working through its diocesan contacts. Often, the educational and lobbying functions of OIJP tend to overlap when dealing with the Church. For example, in 1977 Mr. Henry Brodie, the then international economics advisor of the OIJP, sent legislative data on international financial institutions and human rights to many regional Church offices around the U.S. In the Diocese of New York, where an Office for World Justice and Peace is quite active,* Ms. ALba Zizzamia, its director at the time, explained that the diocese follows through on OIJP information sheets and requests for local grass roots support for particular pieces of

---

*
Within the United States and around the world there are numerous Catholic Offices for World Justice and Peace. These are outgrowths of the Pontifical Commission of Justice and Peace mandated by Pope Paul VI in 1967. They "not only have a role of studying and reflecting on their bishops teaching, but also ɔf reciprocating and sharing their research, studies and experiences in order to promote practical action in defense of the dignity of human person and of his fundamental rights". See: Pontifical Commission of Justice and Peace, The Church and Human Rights (Vatican City: The Commission, 1975). p. 19. They are also mandated to carry out "collaboration with government and NGO's which help to defend and promote human rights". See page 68.

legislation. She stated that the main function of her office, about 90%, was educational and that this job was carried out by the publication of "Notes", a regular newsletteer published five times per year. However, she reported that her office also publishes "Alerts", tear sheets on matters of social concern. She estimated that these latter publicatons are mailed to between five hundred and one thousand members of the diocese, preferably to persons involved in parish councils or influential members of Church social action groups. They, in turn, discuss the "Alerts" with members of their groups, inform them about current legislation and help to rally local concern for specific programs.

In the case of the Brodie memorandum, which dealt with international funancial institutions and human rights, Ms. Zizzamia prepared an "Alert" to be sent out in August of 1977. It explained both the House and the Senate versions of the pending bills on international financial institutions, and its funding in relation to human rights practices. At the same time, it urged support of the Senate version, which Brodie had also recommended in his memorandum, and suggested that people write to members of the conference committee (whose names were

_____

6
Interview with Ms. Alba Zizzamia, January 17, 1980.

listed in the newsletter) to make their wishes known.

The USCC also has its own news service located in its Washington headquarters at 1312 Massachusetts Ave., N.W. Although the service is not required to use any articles sent to it by particular divisions of that organization, OIJP does, in reality, have excellent access to an in-house wire service. At the same time, OIJP also has its own documentation and translation service and makes information available from foreign sources to other members of the human rights network. One such important document which the author came across in the OIJP was the translation of a report on torture in Brazil originally published on July 22, 1970 by the International Commission of Jurists in Geneva. This translation brought to light documents and statements by former Brazilian prisoners, depositions from jails and concentration camps, and evidence of the types of torture that were carried out there. Eventually, such information was passed along the human rights network and found

---

its way into the hearings held by Congressman Fraser in the 1970's.

OIJP works to educate and inform the government about human rights. Its educational function is carried out primarily by Congressional testimony, and by interaction with members of the government. Testimony before Congressional committees is either solicited by a particular member of a committee or offered by the OIJP. Officially, all requests for statements from the government to the OIJP are supposed to be made to the Office of Government Liaison, another department of the USCC. That office is the one which decides if the OIJP will testify at a particular series of hearings and is charged with the responsibility of clearing all testimony before it is given. Very often, however, testimony is solicited informally by a Congressman or a member of his staff who happens to have contact with a particular member of OIJP. In that case, the Director of the OIJP is the one who must give consent for the statement to be given, and must check it for its correctness.

Oftentimes, however, testimony is freely offered by the OIJP on human rights. This occurs when a member of the OIJP staff has particular information which he feels is pertinent to some hearings taking place. In that case, the OIJP member, after getting clearance from the Director, contacts the legislative assistant in charge of a subcommittee and requests to be a witness. These requests are seldom denied, and are usually welcomed. Quigley characterized general USCC-Congressional relations as "increasing", and "improving". He attributed this to two factors. First, he believed that formerly the Church had been concerned with its own institutional well being, but that now it has become more involved in working for peace, justice and other transcendent values. Second, he saw this better relationship resulting from USCC interaction with Congressman Donald Fraser and his Subcommittee on International Organizations and Movements of the House of Reperesentatives. He felt that the hearings held by that subcommittee were key to Congressional receptivity to the Church in the political process in the 1970's. Quigley believed that Fraser challenged the old guard and that he was "more responsive" and "sensitive to the needs of the Catholic community".[8]

Testimony is not given with any regularity, such as once a month. Rather, it depends on what legislation the Congress is dealing with at any particular time. Therefore, testimony is given as the need arises and not considered as the primary job of the OIJP. More important are the day to day activities and opportunities to explain (or teach) about human rights to a broad spectrum of government personnel. This goes beyond Congressional contacts, and includes interaction with members of the State

---

[7] Interview of the author with Mr. Thomas Quigley, December 6, 1980.

[8] Ibid.

Department, the Agency for International Development and even the White House. For example, much of the human rights director's time is spent gathering information, studying legislation and following up on the same. Files revealed numerous meetings, correspondence from White House staff members working on human rights, requests for information and dealings with government personnel, all seeking general knowledge or specific data on human rights. The position of the OIJP with the government during the Carter years was secure enough to warrant White House invitations, such as the one commemorating the Thirtieth Anniversary of the Universal Declaration of Human Rights in 1978,[9] and requests to the Director to address a House subcommittee working group on international affairs.[10]

D. The Lobbying Function

Generally, the term "lobbying" is meant to include any political acitivity carried out by an organized group to support a particular interest. In this study, lobbying is understood to encompass all the political activities of the OIJP on behalf of the American Catholic Church to support the consideration of human rights as a factor in U.S. foreign policy.

9
Held on December 6, 1978.

10
Unpublished notes of address given by Father Bryan Hehir on January 26, 1976 to the Foreign Policy Subcommittee of the International Affairs Working Groups of the House of Representatives.

As Chapter IV has shown, the USCC did not try to influence the government actively from 1968 to 1973 and press for a renewed government concern for human rights. Instead, it acted to inform the media, to gain publicity for the plight of human rights in Latin America, particularly in Brazil, and to develop a grass roots constituency opposed to such repression. It also tried to have an impact on international agencies, such as the OAS, rather than the U.S. government, in order to bring attention to the human rights violations occurring in the Southern Hemisphere. During the years 1968-1973, U.S. government channels were virtually closed to the American and Latin American Churches in their attempts to protest repression. The Nixon Administration had refused to waiver from its policy of "quiet diplomacy" and non-interference in Latin America. Consequently, it was not until the Fraser hearing in 1973, that government receptivity to Catholic political activity on behalf of human rights became accepted and worthwhile. During those hearings, the advice and credible information supplied by the American Catholic Church, through the OIJP, opened the door to more access and better interaction between the government and the Church.

The first Fraser hearings also coincided with the hiring of Father Bryan Hehir in 1973. He continued earlier OIJP efforts on behalf of human rights, and under his direction that department became more involved politically in its cause.

The work of OIJP that falls under the umbrella of lobbying includes giving testimony and statements before the Congress, letter writing, phone calling (blitzing), and private contacts. There are also those actions taken in concert with other specialized human rights groups or coalitions involved in the broad area of international social justice. These cover the entire spectrum of activities generally understood as lobbying; talks with Congressmen and legislative assistants, luncheons, publications and general contacts to persuade influential government personnel to support the human rights stance of USCC and other concerned groups.

Within its own organization, OIJP is assisted in its lobbying efforts by another USCC department, the Office of Government Liaison.[11] Staffed by lobbyists, it first tracks legislation and analyzes it. Second, it keeps the members of the National Conference of Catholic Bishops and the United States Catholic Conference, particularly the OIJP, informed about pending legislation which is of importance to those organizations. Third, it makes contacts with Congressmen and others on Capitol Hill in order to explain the views of the American Catholic Church to the government. Fourth, it lobbies and organizes activities to influence the government. The Office of Government Liaison is also assisted by the Legal Department of the USCC, which interprets and analyzes complex legislation of

---

11
Interview with Mr. Michael Bennett, January 4, 1980.

significance to the Church. It is interesting to note that of the five paid lobbyists employed by the USCC, one of them is charged solely with the responsibility to lobby for human rights.

Within the OIJP, the human rights specialist acts to supplement the work of the Office of Government Liaison and carries out the lobbying function. A sample of lobbying actions in 1977 serves to draw a picture of the original kind of work that was done politically by the OIJP in support of legislation which incorporated respect for itnernational human rights as its underlying principle. Two particular pieces of legislation have been chosen to demonstrate this.

In 1977, OIJP became involved in the preparation and debate of two landmark bills,both of which subsequently passed, concerned with human rights: 1) H 7797, the 1978 Foreign Aid Appropriations Bill and 2) H 5262, the Omnibus Multi-lateral Development Institutions Act. OIJP played a positive role in supporting the human rights provisions of both.

OIJP demonstrated early concern for H 7797 soon after its introduction on 14 June 1977. Within a week of its presentation, on 20 June, Patricia Rengel, the human rights specialist at the time, prepared a letter over the signature of Father Hehir, the OIJP Director, and sent it to all members of the House of Representatives.[12]

12
Letter of Patricia Rengel to the members of the House of Representatives, June 20, 1977. Signed by Father Hehir.

It opposed military aid to Argentina, South Korea, the Philippines and Nicaragua, a move which was being considered favorably by the House at the time. The letter also supported the passage of H 5262 initiated by Congressman Tom Harkin.* That bill required the directors of international financial institutions to turn down loan applications from countries that consistently violated human rights, unless they could be shown to directly help the needy. Harkin's bill was a significant piece of legislation because it tied loans to human rights and the poor. The OIJP letter of 20 June was followed by telephone calls from Mr. Edward Dougherty of the Office of Government Liaison and by Patricia Rengel to members of Congress. They urged support of H 5262 as well as the inclusion of provisions in H 7797 to cut military aid to Argentina, Nicaragua, the Philippines and South Korea.

On 23 June a letter arrived from Father Robert Drinan (D.Mass.), the Catholic priest who was at that time a Representative from Massachusetts. He assured Father Hehir that the text of the OIJP letter that had been sent to the House of Representatives on the 20th had been entered by him into the Congressional Record for the 21st.[13]

---

*
Introduced on March 21, 1977.

[13]
Unpublished letter of Father Drinan to Father Hehir, June 23, 1977.

Work on H 7797 and H 5262 slowed down during the summer of 1977 as Congress recessed. However, on 1 August Patricia Rengel received a letter from Senators Edward Kennedy and Frank Church (D-Idaho) inviting the OIJP to support a new provision to H 7797 which would limit aid to Nicaragua because of its violations of human rights.[14] In response, the OIJP sent each Senator a letter from Father Hehir reiterating the Church's stand on human rights in foreign policy on 4 August.

> ...human rights criterion should be an integral element in the conception, formulation and implementation of U.S. foreign policy. There-fore, we have been and continue to be strongly supportive of all legislative efforts to evaluate U.S. bilateral and multilateral foreign assis-tance in light of the human rights criterion...[15]

During the summer of 1977 Henry Brodie, the international economicst for OIJP at the time, also became involved in lobbying efforts on behalf of the human rights provisions of H 7797 and H 5262. He wrote to the Maryknoll Office of Justice and Peace to encourage Reverend Thomas Marti, director of the Order, to send each member of the Senate a letter protesting aid to the Philippines in light of repression reported by Maryknoll

---

[14]
Unpublished letter of Senators Kennedy and Church to Patricia Rengel on August 1, 1977.

[15]
Letter of Father Hehir to the members of the Senate on August 4, 1977.

missionaries serving in that country.   Marti replied to Brodie's request by writing to the Senators and urging a cut in aid to the Philippines.[16]   Brodie   continued   to work for   the   human   rights sections   of   H 7797.   He followed up with letters   to   diocesan offices   of   Justice   and   Peace,   as   mentioned   earlier,   while encouraging   grass   roots   support   for the Senate version of   most sections of H 7797.

By the fall of 1977,   Legislative work on H 7797 and H   5262 began to start again with the reconvening of Congress.   By early September   most of the provisions of the bills had been   hammered out   and   both   H 7797 and H 5262 were ready to be   discussed   in Conference   Committee.   As   far as H   7797   was   concerned,   the Committee   could   not come to agreement on seven   issues, six   of which   dealt with human rights,   one with trade.   On 6 September Patricia Rengel sent hand delivered letters to all the members of the Conference Committee to support the six specific human rights proposals.[17]   The   Committee continued to debate H 7797   for   more than   a month more.   On 30 September the OIJP,   through Patricia Rengel,   again   wrote to the conferees supporting specific   House and   Senate provisions which,   in OIJP's opinion,   best supported human rights per se in the proposed H 7797.   At the same time,

----

16
Letter of Reverend Thomas Marti to members of the   Senate, undated.

17
Letter of Patricia Rengel to the Members of the Conference Committee, September 6, 1977.

OIJP had continued to work to help in the passage of H 5262 and, in the same letter of 30 September, urged support of Congressman Harkin's bill as well. The OIJP letter stated:

> The USCC wishes to convey to you our grave
> concerns about the threat to vital economic
> multilateral assistance programs posed by
> House amendments to the foreign assistance
> act of 1978, HR 7797 which attaches certain
> conditions to the use of U.S. contributions
> to international financial and other develop-
> ment institutions. *   As you know, the
> the conferees on HR 7797 could not agree on
> these amendments. We urge you to reconsider
> the serious implications of these carefully
> restrictive House amendments and to support
> instead the Senate position which is opposed
> to the denial U.S. contributions to multi-
> lateral agencies for 1) assistance to seven
> specified developing countries and 2) projects
> to expand palm oil, citrus or sugar production...
> We fully suppport the application of human rights
> criteria to the operations of multilateral
> assistance agencies, however, we believe the
> appropriate way to do this is by requiring
> U.S. executive directors to international
> financial institutions to oppose loans or
> other assistance to countries guilty of
> gross violations of human rights except
> for programs which clearly serve the
> basic needs of the people as provided
> by the Harkin Amendment HR 5262....
> We also support the application of human
> rights criteria to U.S. bilateral aid
> programs. Prohibitions or reductions of
> bilateral aid to specifically designated
> countries, we believe is an appropriate
> way to apply these criteria since such
> action has no adverse multilateral
> implications. We therefore support House

---

*
The House tried to restrict the financial activities of the
World Bank, making loans dependent on respect for human rights.
The Senate, President Carter, and the OIJP opposed this after
Robert McNamara, the Bank's President,said that the World Bank
could not accept contributions with political strings attached.

> amendments to eliminate or curtail U.S.
> military assistance to such countries as
> Argentina, Brazil, El Salvador, Uruguay
> and the Philippines. The severity of
> human rights repression in these countries
> is well documented. Moreover, since the
> aid is military, not economic, there is a
> strong presumption that it will be used
> to support efforts to violate human rights. 18

On 3 October 1977 Congressman Harkin's international financial institutions bill, H 5262, was signed into law as the Omnibus Multilateral Development Institutions Act. It was important because, for the first time, international loans would be tied to respect for human rights. The law also provided enough flexibility to allow loans to countries which violated human rights, if it could be shown that those loans would directly benefit the needy. Thus, American monetary policy was designed, finally, to help the poor and place sanctions on those nations in which repression was tolerated or encouraged. Shortly thereafter, on 19 October 1977, President Carter also signed H 7797 into law as the 1978 Foreign Appropriations Act. Human rights principles were an underlying consideration of this law which 1)limited military aid and credit sales to the Philippines, 2) prohibited direct U.S. aid to Viet Nam, Cambodia, Laos, Cuba, Angola and Mozambique, 3) denied military aid to Ethiopia and Uruguay, and 4) prohibited military credit sales to Brazil, El Salvador, Guatamala and Argentina.

18
Letter of Patricia Rengel to the Conference Committee on H 7797, September 30, 1977. Signed by Father Hehir.

The successful lobbying effort of OIJP on behalf of the specific human rights provisions of both H 7797 and H 5262 was an indication of the ability of the American Catholic Church to utilize its resources and play a positive role in the passage of legislation based on a respect for human rights. These two successes are in contrast to the Church's record between 1973 and 1976. There are few other documented exampled in the files of OIJP, before 1977,* to demonstrate a history of intense political activity on behalf of human rights legislation. With the exception of 1977, it would seem that during the years 1973 to 1978, the years during which Congress wrote most of the human rights legislation, OIJP played a minimal lobbying role.

In the past the OIJP has, on occasion, requested that members of the Catholic hierarchy testify before Congressional committees investigating human rights. The prestigious position of such individuals within the Church adds credence to the information being provided and serves to underscore the importance that the Church attaches to the consideration of human rights in U.S. foreign policy. However, over the years, only John Cardinal Deardon, the Archbishop of Detroit, Bishop Peter Gerety of Newark, Father Theodore Hesburg, the President of Notre Dame, some other Presidents of Catholic universities, and missionaries have been asked to testify. The OIJP has made only limited use of the upper eschelons of the Catholic clergy to give

---

* Prior to 1977, human rights was not a specialized desk at OIJP.

weight to their lobbying attempts on behalf of human rights legislation.

Private contacts are also used, at times, as a means of lobbying by the OIJP. While some anti-Catholics have alluded to clergymen pressuirng Catholic Representatives and Senators to vote the Catholic "partyline" on particular pieces of legislation,[19] this has been denied unequivocally by leaders at the USCC. The official policy of OIJP has been to refrain from pressuring Congressmen because of their religious affiliation.[20] Correspondence about legislation, phone calls between staff personnel, and attendance at briefings and hearings, are all part of the way that political contacts are made in Washington. The OIJP works like any other interest group within this system of Capitol Hill rituals to meet and influence individuals who could be of assistance to the Church on specific matters of human rights legislation. USCC lobbyists insist that contacts are made by simply knocking on Congressmen's doors and introducing themselves to staff personnel.[21] It is possible to conclude, then, that the Catholic religious beliefs of Congressmen are not used by the OIJP as the basis for applying extra pressure or expecting adherence to a Catholic "partyline".

19
  See Paul Blanshard, American Freedom and Catholic Power (Boston: The Beacon Press, 1949).

20
  Interview with Father Hehir, January 4, 1980.

21
  Interview with Michael Bennett, January 4, 1980.

While Congressional receptivity to the political activities of the Catholic Church began with the Fraser hearings in 1973, it was not until 1977 that the Catholic Church was able to increase its contacts and access to the White House. In April of 1977, Bishop Joseph Bernardin wrote to the President, Jimmy Carter, on behalf of the National Conference of Catholic Bishops in regard to the question of human rights. He wrote:

> ...[We] pledge to continue speaking out
> on human rights whenever they are violated
> at home or abroad. We will do all we can
> to convince our members they should be in
> the forefront of those speaking in defense
> of and acting for the fulfillment of the
> rights of men and women at the local,
> national, and international level. 22

Five days later Bishop Kelly, Secretary General of the USCC, wrote to Vice President Mondale, "...human rights is a central concern of the Church". [23] One month later, in May of 1977, the official decision to base foreign policy on human rights was unveiled by President Carter at Notre Dame.

Interaction between the OIJP and government flowed easily during the Carter Administration. In April of 1977, the human rights specialist of the OIJP was invited to the White House for a human rights briefing. [24] In March 1978, Patricia Derian,

---

22
Unpublished letter of Bishop Bernardin to President Carter, April 7, 1977.

23
Unpublished letter of Bishop Kelly to Vice President Mondale, April 12, 1977.

24
Unpublished memo of Patricia Rengel to Father Hehir appraising him of the invitation, April 21, 1977.

Assistant Secretary for Human Rights and Humanitarian Affairs of the State Department, held a luncheon to discuss human rights and included the OIJP human rights specialist.[25] In July of 1978 Joyce Starr, the White House human rights advisor, asked the Catholic Church, through the OIJP, to support the President's statements on behalf of Anatoly Scharansky and Eli Ginzburg.[26]

Father Hehir also used the improving executive OIJP contacts to work for human rights. In April 1977, he sent open letters to the members of the State Department calling for a "stop to security assistance, especially military programs",[27] to Argentina. In November, Hehir wrote to Secretary of State Vance advising him of the information the OIJP had been receiving about unwarranted arrests and disappearances in Argentina.[28] In December, Hehir received a response from the State Department advising him that Secretary Vance would continue to "press the Argentines on actions to protect the dignity of the person and

---

25
    Unpublished letter of Patricia Derian to Patricia Rengel, March 17, 1978.

26
    Unpublished letter of Joyce Starr to Patricia Rengel, July 18, 1978.

27
    Letter of Father Hehir to members of the State Department, October 11, 1977.

28
    Letter of Father Hehir to Cyrus Vance, November 17, 1977.

the rule of law".[29] The letter also discussed interventions on behalf of particular individuals whose names must be protected.

The use of private contacts in lobbying for human rights is supplemented by OIJP work in coalition with specialized agencies dedicated to influencing the government, in a general way, on international social concerns. Two such groups with which the OIJP cooperates for lobbying purposes are the Washington Office on Latin America (WOLA), and the Coalition for a New Foreign and Defense Policy. Gathering information, supplying data to the members of the human rights network, publishing statements,giving testimony, and coordinating the political activities of several religious organizations concerned about various problems in Latin America are the tasks of these organizations. The Coalition for a New Foreign and Defense Policy has a special Human Rights Working Group in which the OIJP participates.

III. Factors which limited the Role of the American Catholic Church in the Development of U.S. Human Rights Policy During the 1970's.

During the 1970's, American Catholic efforts to advance international human rights were positive, but limited. Four key factors were at work which tended to minimize the effectiveness of the Church in these areas. First, the Catholic Church had

---

29
    Letter of Mr. Robert W. Zimmerman, Director of East Coast Affairs of the State Department to Father Hehir, December 6, 1977.

committed itself to a diverse number of issues, and had, therefore, diluted its capacity to influence the government on behalf of human rights legislation. Second, there was minimal hierarchial support for OIJP efforts in the area of human rights. Third, the unique international position of the Church mitigated against its ability to work for human rights. And fourth, Church leaders were uncertain as to what political role, if any, the Church should play in its efforts to promote human rights.

A. Commitment to a Diverse Number of Issues

As the decade of the 70's unfolded, the new Director of the OIJP, Father Bryan Hehir, committed his office to cover a broad spectrum of issues. And indeed, OIJP has become involved in many matters in the international arena since that time. A summary of OIJP legislative activity in the year 1977 alone indicated its involvement, not only in matters of human rights, but in U.S. food assistance programs, the International Development Fund, the Panama Canal Treaties, the boycott of South African chrome (repeal of the Byrd Amendment), and disarmament. [33] This was not to

---

[33]
See the "Summary of Legislative Activity of OIJP for 1977", Office of International Justice and Peace (United States Catholic Conference: Washington, D.C., January, 1978.

mention other work on matters concerned with the   Mid-East,   or

Communism,   or   involvement   in   coalitions   with   various   other

religious   groups concerned for Latin America,   and other matters

which   the Bishops brought to the office of OIJP at   other   given

times.

This trend toward more involvement in diverse issues by OIJP

was   expected to continue into the 1980's.   Father   Hehir's   own

legislative   forecast called for expansion into the areas of pro-

life   activities   as they related to U.S.   population   policy   in

developing countries,   SALT,   and women's rights.[34]   In   reality,

however,   Central   America,   and   human   rights   problems   in   El

Salvador and Nicaragua pervaded every aspect of OIJP's activities

during   the 1980's and narrowed rather than broadened,   the focus

of its interests.   Thus, one of its limiting factors disappeared

due to the necessities of the times, resulting in a strengthening

of its influence in the area of human rights.

---

*
During the Iranian hostage crisis,   OIJP was charged with
managing Church policy on the issue.   Much of Hehir's personal
time has been involved with this matter.   In fact,he accompanied
Bishop Gumbleton when he visited the hostages for   Christmas in
1979.   Such matters also dilute the amount of time that can be
given to any one issue.

34
Unpublished prospectus of future missions,   objectives use
of personnel and outlook of legislative activity.   Department of
Social   Development   and World   Peace,   Office   of   International
Justice and Peace, Plans and Programs, 1979.

B. Lack of Adequate Hierarchial Support

Another significant reason for limited Catholic influence in the area of human rights during the 1970's stemed from the fact that the American Bishops in the NCCB (who actually are responsible for making the policy which is carried out by the USCC), had not, themselves, given strong enough support for human rights. While Congressman Harkin called for grass roots support for human rights,his legislative assistant wrote that "this would take direction from the top of the American hierarchy, which has not yet been forthcoming".[35]

Such a lack of leadership was also borne out by Father Louis Colonnese, who headed the Latin American Division of the USCC from 1968 until he was fired in 1971. When asked what priority human rights had during his tenure as director of international affairs for USCC he replied: "Top-number one priority. Though I did not believe that [the] bishops were opposed to human rights, nonetheless the issue gave rise to many conflicts".[36] He went on to explain the source of these problems:

> When you approach the question of human rights
> as our State Department does (with regard to
> U.S. interests etc.), then you're bound to have
> conflict with those who approach the issue from
> a strictly biblical reference. 37

---

[35]
Correspondence with Miss Holly Burkthaler, March 11, 1980.

[36]
Correspondence of Louis Colonnese with the author, October 29, 1980.

[37]
Ibid.

Colonnese believed that, although his office tried to pursue international human rights from a purely religious posture, the moral concerns of the Bishops were tinged with political considerations. In another conversation, he said that in the late 1960's the American Bishops were "overcautious", "fearful", and "insecure in rooting their social action", on behalf of human rights, in the political process.[38] Further, he said that he felt that the Bishops were afraid to "disrupt the course of events in foreign policy" because they did not want to upset the domestic gains that had been made by the Catholic Church in the matter of federal aid to private education in the 1960's.[39]

Colonnese also criticized the Bishops in later correspondence. He opposed cooperation between the Catholic hierarchy and the government on matters of human rights which had political overtones. Specifically, he disapproved the Bishop's tacit acceptance of the government's definition of who is a political refugee and who may be admitted into the U.S. He said that the Bishops supported the government's policy of granting residence to refugees from leftist regimes, such as Cuba, but not from right wing governments, such as El Salvador. Colonnese charged that if the Bishops "were to be a faithful witness to the human rights of all people....the Church would have to change its

---

38
Conversation with Louis Colonnese, October 19, 1980.

39
Ibid.

institutional life style".⁴⁰   He wrote: "I think the Bishops are not prepared to make this change".⁴¹

Finally, he summed up his feelings:

> While a few American bishops have made some
> valuable statements on human rights; while
> others have concretized the teaching in
> visible witness to human rights (Bishops
> supporting boycotts, etc.) yet I _feel_
> the hierarchial structure of the Church
> has generally remained in the area of
> rhetoric rather than reality.⁴²

Colonnese's criticism had some validity in fact.   Since the inception of the National Conference of Catholic Bishops in 1966, there had been very few statements from the American hierarchy about human rights. After World War II, some public condemnation of religious persecution in Eastern Europe was made by the National Catholic Welfare Conference. After the inception of the NCCB, and the mandate of Vatican II, it was expected that the Bishops would become more involved in international social justice matters.   In 1967, they did establish a Secretariat for World Justice and Peace but, short of calling for the pursuit of international development, took little significant action in this area.   It was not until 1976, when the Bishops sponsored a meeting for laymen to make some of their concerns known, that the

---

40
Correspondence Colonnese, _op. cit._, p. 3.

41
 Ibid.

42
 Ibid.

issue again received some recognition. However, no significant policy statement on human rights came out of a later 1976 meeting of the Bishops called to act on the suggestions of the laymen in social justice and dogmatic matters. In 1977, the Bishops did issue a statement entitled "Religious Liberty in Eastern Europe". That document stressed the right to religious freedom in Communist countries, and also finally spoke out favorably in support of the Final Act of the Helsinki Accords. In a background statement, it scored the U.S. government for conducting U.S. foreign policy with a human rights concern that was "ill-defined and ambiguous".[43] In 1978, the National Conference of Catholic Bishops, at their annual meeting, again expressed general hopes for the advancement of human rights, but offered nothing specific in this regard. In fact, they voted to postpone action on censuring South Africa and also delayed taking any stand on the Equal Rights Amendment as well.

Such a lack of leadership and consensus on important moral/political matters was, partially, the result of the diverse views within the Church. Conservatives and Liberals among the hierarchy were not able to reach agreement on significant matters

---

[43]
National Council of Catholic Bishops, "Religious Liberty in Eastern Europe, A Test for Human Rights", (Washington: The United States Catholic Conference, 1977), p. 16.

of international and domestic import. Consequently, they left the Church membership without any action guides to work for social justice.

Again, this situation was resolved by time and circumstances beyond the Bishop's control. The particular turning point seemed to come as a result of several dramatic events: the continued, systematic persecution of Catholics in El Salvador culminating in the rape and murder of five Church women, and the election of Ronald Reagan in 1980. Both situations polarized the Catholic hierarchy in America with regard to human rights. Ambivalence was replaced by activism and a resolve to protect the human rights of all individuals by everyone and all means possible, even political activity.

C. Unique International Position of the Church

Another reason for restrained American Catholic involvement on behalf of human rights in the last decade had resulted from the unique position of the Church within the international community. Highly visible and vulnerable to attack, the American Catholic Church must constantly weight the possible effects of its activities on behalf of human rights on the Church in other countries. Often the American Catholic Church has had to play a cautious role in its denunciation of repressive regimes, as in

---

44
    For a discussion of the current hierarchial schism between liberal and conservative ideas among the U.S. Catholic Bishops see: Thomas Fleming, "Divided Shepards of a Restive Flock", New York Times Magazine, 16 January 1977, pp. 9, 34-39, 42 and 44.

the case of Uganda, and minimize its recommendations for bilateral and multilateral aid, in order to protect the safety of many of its members abroad. In a letter from Congrssman Harkin's legislative assistant to the author, [45] certain priests were named as having supported human rights and as having worked with the Congressman in this area. However, it was requested that the identities of these Jesuits and Maryknolls be kept secret in order to protect them from possible jeopardy and reprisal in their missionary posts.

The Church has been and remains in a unique position, different from other U.S. or international non-governmental organizaitons. Because the Church has been allied with political parties in other countries, criticism of regimes by the American Catholic Church is often interpreted as criticism that is politically motivated. At the same time, many members of the Catholic clergy abroad are not only outspoken about political repression, but are themselves activists and in the forefront of activities to weaken or overthrow such regimes. The American Catholic Church, then ,must maintain silence in order to protect the physical security of these people, and the Church, or risk causing them jeopardy. Amnesty International, or the International Commission of Jurists, are more able to make accusations against political regimes without being condemned for political or religious bias because their members are less visible or vulnerable to systematic government retaliation.

45
Burkthaler, op. cit., p. 1.

In such cases where the safety of the entire religious community is at stake, the American Catholic Church can only support human rights endeavors in an unpolitical way. Often the Church has served as an intermediary between the persecuted and those in power. The files of the OIJP contain numerous letters to Latin American Ambassadors, U.S. Congressmen and members of the State Department urging action on behalf of specific persons charged with political crimes. They are usually protests against the treatment of clergy, but at other times they also advocate clemency and release for political "criminals". In short, much of the work of OIJP must necessrarily be non-political and done behind the scenes in order to be effective and safe.

D. Church Uncertainly About Its Political Role

Finally, limited Church involvement in human rights also resulted from the uncertainly within the Church during the 1970's about what role it should be playing, generally, in the political process. Father Hehir discussed this normative issue with the author in 1980 and the philosopy discussed then, was prologue to the political action which actually occurred later. Hehir believed that the Church should function in a dual role: as improver of the community and as moral teacher. As a secondary consequence, he believed that the Church must often get involved in the political process in order to carry out these responsibilities effectively.

In the first role as improver of the community, Hehir believed that it was the Church's duty to aid people in the performance of reponsible functions. By helping to shape viewpoints, perspectives, activities and choices of the whole body of people, he contended that the Church can form a "vision of community", and create a moral atmosphere "touching the end of public opinion".[46] This role, as Hehir perceived it, was related to the Church's responsibility to form conscience. And, in conversation with Hehir, it was clear that the priest felt that the way to carry out the principles of the conscience into reality was by the use of the political process. In the matter of human rights, Hehir said that substantive facts were often presented by the OIJP in the course of its political activity for the purpose of providing information necessary to clarify moral alternatives and perspectives, and to explain the moral, not merely the political, implications of particular public policies. Hehir believed that by doing this, the Church could create an atmosphere in which people, through their government representatives, could respond to international communal needs within the framework of transcendental values, rather than mere political interests.

In the second role, Hehir envisioned the Church as a repository of moral wisdom garnered from revelation and two thousand years of reflection. Because of its vast experience,

---

46
Interview with Father Hehir, January 4, 1980.

Hehir believed that the Church should deal not only with religious matters, but with social and cultural questions as well. In its capacity as moral teacher, Hehir argued that the Church should exercise its role as moral guide by constantly participating in the public policy debate. Thus, he justified OIJP monitoring, educational, and political activity on behalf of human rights and other political/moral questions.

The underlying assumption in this view is that the Church has a part to play in the moral development of man, and that such a vital role cannot be abrogated to the State. This outlook assumes that the interests of the State will always capitulate to the selfish needs of the community if the Church does not prod the State to commit itself to transcendent values. By taking an active role in directing the consciences of individuals and activities of groups to influence the policies of the government, this view postulates that the Church can make a contribution to assure that more humane and civilized activity will be pursued by the State. Within this school of thought, the end of religion is considered broad enough to justify Church action to influence social, cultural and political policy. More importantly, here,is the supposition that the Church should use political means to instruct and shape public policy. While many argue that the pulpit is the place where conscience should be formed, the Church in the 1970's, was already emphasizing the need for political action to assure such transcendent goals.

Indeed, Hehir characterized the first three years of his work at OIJP (which paralleled the first government attempts to write human rights legislation) as a time when his office worked for the implementation of a principle, not a particular law or set of laws. According to him, one of the main concerns of OIJP from 1973 on was to see that human rights became a factor in the foreign policy equation. To that end OIJP, under his direction, became involved with the Fraser hearings "from the beginning".[47] Because Hehir understood and identified the human rights issue as essentially moral in content, he wanted the NCCB to be involved and in the forefront of the movement. He requested that the past President of that body, John Cardinal Deardon, testify along with himself and Tom Quigley at the first hearings. The tone and involvement on that issue set the pattern for OIJP activity to instill a concern for human rights into American public policy. From the Fraser hearings on, Hehir chose to testify at all Congressional hearings where he felt OIJP could have an impact on human rights legislation.

His guidelines were quite simple: 1) to choose cases where OIJP had substantial documentation of alleged human rights violations, 2) to testify where U.S. foreign policy had some relationship to human rights, and 3) to act only where local churches had made their feelings known and would not be compromised by American Church criticism of repressive regimes.

47
Ibid.

Thus, Brazil, Chile and Argentina were early targets of OIJP testimony to assure that their compliance with human rights standards would be a criteria for the reception of U.S. economic and military aid. It also explains why the American Catholic Church did not become more deeply involved in other countries where repression did occur, but where it did not have enough information or was asked not to do anything overt, as in the case of Uganda.

This view was counterbalanced by others within the Church in the 1970's who saw politics as being outside the proper realm of Catholic institutional or social interests. In the United States one member of the hierarchy who espoused this opinion was Bishop Peter Gerety, the past Archbishop of the Diocese of Newark. Having served as chairman of the justice subcommittee of the Bicentennial Committee of the NCCB, Gerety said that he believed that neither the Bishops nor their episcopal organization, the NCCB, should play any political role.[48] Rather, he stated, there were influences which the Church could and should exert, but only in the formation of individual conscience, not in the development of public policy. Gerety believed that the citizen should act on his own beliefs developed by religious teachings, and that Church

---

48
    Interview with Archbishop Peter Gerety, February 8, 1980. The Archbishop also declared that he was instrumental in cutting the meetings of the NCCB from twice yearly to an annual conference. He also made reference to the New Jersey Catholic Conference whenever the question of Church politics arose. He clearly did not want anything to do with political activity or influence.

influence in political matters should be indirect. In no uncertain terms, the Archbishop said, "We strictly try to stay out of partisan politics".[49] He claimed that the Church should speak out on issues,not candidates, on principles, but not on specific legislation.

This opinion represented the other view of the normative question as to whether or not the Church should participate in the American political arena. The underlying assumption in this view is that there are dangers about direct involvement in politics, and that the Church should stay above the political fray. It suggests that to become involved in the political process compromises the essential goodness and holiness of the Church. Further, in this view, the Church is perceived principally as a spiritual entity; its organization only an expedient means to carry out its religious function. Indeed, in this school of thought, the role of the Church in society is interpreted rather narrowly, that is, as the formulator of consciences in strictly "moral" or "dogmatic" matters. Church responsibility to insure the implementation of specific social, economic or political principles is minimized, and the role of the citizen in these areas is stressed.

At the same time, this attitude has a healthy respect for the intelligence and competence of the citizen to act responsibly on matters of political/moral importance. While the role of the

---

49
  Ibid.

Church in politics is perceived as passive and indirect in this view, the Church member acting as citizen, is expected to accomplish the moral ends of religion by his participation in the political process. Purposeful lobbying is not looked upon as a proper function of the institutional Church in this school of thought. Indeed the Church is not envisioned as simply another pressure group in this view. Rather, it is very sensitive to the influence which it has over its members. The Reverend Wipfler of the NCC told the author that the role of any Church should be to raise political/moral issues to the level of visibility, but that to use the authority of religion to push people to a particular action "is very serious".[50]

Finally, this attitude also affords the Church the comfortable position of being able to sit in judgment on political policies and practices which it did not initiate or condone. In this view, the Church is perceived as an impartial critic of the actions of the State, as the "conscience" of the government.

Such differences of opinion on the normative question of whether or not the Church should become involved in the political process hampered Catholic efforts to work for the inclusion of the principle of human rights into American foreign policy during the 1970's. Compounded with factors mentioned earlier; the

---

[50] Interview with Reverend Wipfler, January 14, 1980.

diverse interests of the Church, the lack of hierarchial support for human rights and the position of the Church within the international community, it is now possible to understand more clearly why the role of the American Catholic Church in the formulation of U.S. foreign policy was limited prior to the 1980's.

V. Conclusion

In retrospect, it is evident that there are three definite functions that the American Catholic Church can perform to advance international human rights. Two of these functions are less directly political; monitoring human rights violations around the globe and educating or informing the media, the public and the government about world repression. The performance of both of these functions can serve to help create a climate of concern and a constituency dedicated to taking action to work for the consideration of human rights as a factor in U.S. foreign policy. The third function, lobbying, is more clearly a political task, and such action has the potential of impressing the views of the American Catholic Church on U.S. foreign aid legislation and other policy matters.

During the 1970's the Church made an important, if limited, contribution to the formulation of American human rights foreign policy. Its modest contribution is understandable, however, in light of the discussion of those factors that acted to minimize

Catholic efforts on behalf of human rights. The commitment of the OIJP to diverse international issues, the lack of hierarchial support for human rights, the position of the Church in the world, and the normative debate of the role of the Church in politics have all hampered the effectiveness of the Church in its efforts to advance international human rights. Very significantly, these problems were for the most part resolved in the 1980's as the Church became more directly involved in the political process.

CHAPTER VI: QUESTIONS FOR THE FUTURE

The   decade of the 1980's raised some fundamental   questions
about   the   nature of   the   U.S.   Catholic   Church/State   dynamic.
Indeed,   what ethical,   empirical, prudential recommendations can
be   made with regard to the political role of the   U.S.   Catholic
Church and American human rights foreign policy?

A.   The Ethical Question: Should the Church be Involved
in Politics?

The   decision of the Church since Vatican II to enlarge   its
responsibilities   to include social justice concerns,   now places
new   obligations on the American Catholic Church.   It   must   now
speak   and act,   as well as find and use the most effective means
to   facilitate   social   change   within   society.   The   American
Catholic   Church   must also reassess its relationship   with   U.S.
power   groups and institutions now in order to work   harmoniously
with them to bring about social justice.   In short,   the   Church
must   accept   its   social   justice   mandate,   use   its   improving
political   position with the United States,   and become   involved
increasingly   in   the   U.S.   political process.   It must join in
coalition   with other non-governmental groups to   advance   social
justice   goals such as human rights.   For,   there is no way that
the   Church   can have a major impact on the development   of   U.S.
foreign   policy without   working   with,   and   participating   in,
American   politics   to   make   its   views   and   values   known.
Congressman Thomas Harkin,   author of several significant   pieces

of human rights legislation, agreed with the author when he said that the Church as a "legitimate right to make known its moral stand".[1] Furthermore, he recommended that the Church use routine political lobbying tactics to attain such ends and chided the USCC for not playing more of a political role to advance international human rights.[2]

Father Bryan Hehir, Director of the Office of International Justice and Peace of the USCC, and others in the USCC clearly perceive of the Church as more than a religious institution today. They reflect the attitude of the author and a growing number of people, currently, who perceive of religious organizations, especially the U.S. Catholic Church, as special interest groups. However, instead of representing oil, or the auto industry, or the banks, religious organizations represent the interests of the poor, the abused, the deprived and the neglected around the world. It is the responsibility of the Church to provide a voice for those who cannot speak for themselves in the political arena. In short, it is the responsibility of the Church to bring social justice concerns, such as human rights, to the public policy debate by political means in order to strike a balance of interests in the formulation of U.S. foreign policy.

---

[1]
Interview with Congressman Thomas Harkin, February 19, 1980.

[2]
Ibid.

During the Reagan Administration, U.S. foreign policy has been designed to restrict the importance of human rights as a factor in U.S. international relations. The President's advisors early on recommended that:

> Internal policy-making procedures should be structured to insure that the human rights area is not in a position to paralyze or unduly delay decisions on issues where human rights concerns conflict with other vital U.S. interest. [3]

Since taking office, Reagan had been minimizing human rights as a consideration in U.S. foreign policy, emphasizing instead the validity of Executive intentions to stop Communist subversion in this hemisphere. In an attempt to be "pragmatic", and "moderate",[4] and more realistic, the U.S. government had not only resumed, but stepped up, aid to El Salvador and other nations which consistently violated human rights. If the Church does not represent the moral interest in foreign policy by political action, who will?

B.   The Empirical Question: Can the Church Avoid Complacency and Dogmatism?

Clearly, there are also two dangers that face the Church as it participates in the political process to work for human rights: dogmatism and complacency. As the American Catholic

---

[3]
Juan de Onis, "Reagan's State Dept. Latin Team Asks Curbs on 'Social Reformers'", New York Times,,4 December, 1950, p. 17.

[4]
Phillip Tubman, "At the Pentagon and State Department: Pragmatic Tone", New York Times, 2 March 1980, p. 1 and 8.

Church becomes more directly and aggressively involved in politics to advance human rights, can it avoid the temptation of advancing its own dogmatic views by political means? There are two reasons why such a possibility is becoming remote. First, the American Catholic Church has built a solid base of political action committed to social justice rather than dogmatic concerns since the 1970's, and second, the American political process has demonstrated its ability to rebuff attempts to legislate dogmatic interests in the past.

Since Vatican II, the American Catholic Church has shown its ability to work within the American political process as one institution among many to support the broad social justice goals mandated by that Council. The Church has been able to work for social justice during the 1970's and apply political pressure for that end in the 1980's. During that time, the Church has continued to work with the NCC and other special interest groups, both religious and non-religious, all of whom are dedicated to incorporating the principle of respect for human rights into U.S. foreign policy. The American Catholic Church is currently a member of such inter-denominational organizations as the Washington Office on Latin America, and works with the Quakers, B'nai B'rith, and other NGOs sincerely attempting to advance international human rights. In short, the American Catholic Church has demonstrated a record of ecumenism, cooperation and a willingness to participate in the political arena just as any other special interest group for broad social justice concerns.

The American Catholic Church has displayed its good faith, credibility, and social concern before the Fraser Committee, and it has lobbied for specific pieces of human rights legislation during the last two decades. This study has shown that the Church has built a solid base of social concern and a political network to support the conclusion that the Church can function within the American political arena without slipping into dogmatism.

At the same time, however, a safeguard does exist to counter dogmatism if the American Catholic Church does try to advance its religious ideas politically. It is the open forum of the U.S. political arena, which serves to check the power of any one interest group within the political process. Indeed, history has shown, that when American Catholicism had demanded privileged status, or sought dogmatic or institutional interests which were clearly in opposition to American constitutional principles, the Church was rebuffed within the political arena. The repudiation of Al Smith, the challenge of Myron Taylor and Mark Clark, and the denial of federal aid to parochial schools, all confirm the ability of the American political process to withstand a Catholic "dogmatic incursion" should that occur.

What is a more serious danger, in the author's opinion, is the second pitfall of a lack of Church political activity: the possibility that the Church will succumb to complacency in advancing social justice goals such as human rights. Indeed, if the Church chooses not to pursue the most effective means to bring about a change in the course of U.S. foreign policy or political activity, why should it be assumed that it would choose to carry out a less fruitful type of non-political activity to advance social justice concerns? The Church can avoid this danger by recognizing its non-political activities as a means to support and solidify political activity by others. Although it may choose not to involve inself directly by political means to advance its social justice goals, it can work to encourage a constituency to act politically on behalf of those in need of social justice. Thus, the Church can recognize itself not as a special interest group but as a stimulus by informing, prodding, encouraging, and jolting the general public and the media to enter and influence the political arena on behalf of such issues as human rights.

However, the Church cannot go back: it can never abrogate the political responsibility it has taken during the last two decades to work for social justice. It cannot and will not simply withdraw from the American political arena, for to do so would be to make its work harder, less beneficial, and less meaningful.

At the same time, it would leave voiceless the victims of repression who have come to depend on the Church to speak for them in a political forum that allows such an organization to participate for the good of mankind.

C. The Prudential Question: What More Can the Church do Safely, to Advance Human Rights?

This book has clearly shown both non-political and political actions that the Church can take to advance international human rights. Of an indirect political nature, the functions of monitoring and educating are two particularly valuable services that the Church can perform to keep human rights abuses visible before the general public, the media and the government. The Church can, and must, do more in this area than it has in the past, especially in light of the Reagan legacy of de-emphasis on human rights. The Church's commitment to a diverse number of international issues should not and need not prevent bolder and more intense non-political activity by that institution to keep the matter of human rights visible. More press releases, interviews, briefings, articles, news conferences, and statements by the Church could serve to keep alive the constituency for human rights that the Church had created in the late 1960's and 1970's. At the same time the Church can also repeat its appeal to international organizations to redress repression if the

United States government will not. It can bring more cases before the OAS and expand such activities by protesting before the United Nations Human Rights Commission as well. The Church can also work more closely with the larger NGO's dedicated to human rights, such as Amnesty International, the International Commission of Jurists, and the Red Cross. In coalition with these special interest groups, all of which have developed a certain expertise in working for human rights during the last decade, the Church can be more effective in making an impact on a public becoming more complacent daily about human rights as it is encouraged to support a foreign policy based on a response to the spread of Communism in this hemisphere. The Church must continue its old alliances such as that with the National Council of Churches, and seek stronger ties with new ones in order to present and ecumenical front willing to oppose repression. Religious groups will have to band together again, as they did in the beginning of the last decade, to pool their information and resources if they are to be effective today to support international human rights. The Churches represent the best means of keeping communications open and obtaining information from other parts of the world about repression, and they must bring this news to the public again.

The hierarchy must also play a stronger role in support of human rights. The National Conference of Catholic Bishops must use the weight and prestige of its organization to speak out and take action to oppose international repression. Statements of solidarity with the clergy in countries where human rights are violated, should be made by the entire body of Catholic Bishops at their annual meetings. At the same time, the hierarchy should spell out specific guidelines for the advancement of human rights. These should include allotments of money to publicize repression in the media, the establishment of a human rights forum similar to that of CICOP which existed from 1963-1973, and support for political activity to impress the importance of such concerns on the government.

Of a more directly political nature, the Church has several options that it can exercise to be more effective to bring the human rights issue back into the political arena. First, it can make better use of its own internal organization to disseminate information and rally grass roots support for human rights. In the past, diocesan contacts were used infrequently and without much regard for the potential influence they could exert on their legislators. The Church, through the OIJP, must make better use of local parish contacts and encourage them to mount massive letter writing campaigns to influence their Congressman to remain concerned about human rights. Second, the OIJP can be expanded to better carry out the political activities of the Church on behalf of human rights. One human rights specialist employed in that Department and one lobbyist hired by the Office of Government Liaison cannot possibly carry out the important human rights work of the entire American Catholic Church. Although their efforts are supplemented by others within their departments, in reality, there are literally only two people who are committed full time to working politically for human rights for the American Catholic Church. More staff personnel should be hired to make contacts on Capitol Hill with new Congressmen, to give more testimony before legislative hearings on foreign aid, and to track legislation which is now deterimental to maintaining human rights as a factor in U.S. foreign policy. In short, the Church must redouble its political activity to keep human rights concerns alive.

The Church has come a long way since its concerns were merely institutional, its ideas un-American, its function simply religious, its acceptability questionable, and its power limited. It has overcome the obstacles of political isolation and internal authoritarianism, and has begun a new era of ecumenism and social justice action in the United States. These successes portend a future of increased Church non-political and political activity to work for the betterment of mankind and the establishment of more civilized criteria in the formulation of U.S. foreign policy by the advancement of international human rights. It is the author's hope, in the matter of human rights, that the State will never allow repression to go unchallanged for the sake of political expediency; and that the Church will never abrogate its political responsibility to bring about social justice to accommodate the winds of political change.

APPENDIX

U.S. BISHOPS
ADVISORY COUNCIL

Social Concerns   Canonical Affairs

U.S.C.C.   N.C.C.B.

Administrative Committee   Administrative Committee

Executive Committee   Executive Committee

Departments   Standing Committees   Ad Hoc Committees
(Twenty Three)

Communications   Education   Social Justice
(3 sub-units)   (7 sub-units)   and World Peace

Domestic   Office of
Social   International
Development   Justice and
Peace

BIBLIOGRAPHY

BIBLIOGRAPHY

I.   PUBLISHED INFORMATION
     A.   BOOKS

Abbott, Walter, ed. The Documents of Vatican II. New
      York: Herder and Herder, 1966.

Adams, James. The Growing Church Lobby in Washington.
      Grand Rapids, Michigan: William B. Eerdmans, 1970.

Barrett, Patricia. Religious Liberty and the American
      Presidency. New York: Herder and Herder, 1963.

Belfrage, Cecil. The American Inquisition, 1945-1960.
      Indianapolis: Bobbs-Merrill, 1973.

Bender, Margaret and Blaise Levai, eds. Human Rights.
      Cincinnati, Ohio: The United Methodist Church, 1968.

Berkouwer, G.C. The Second Vatican Council and the New
      Catholicism. Grand Rapids, Michigan: William Eerdmans,
      1965.

Billington, Ray Allen. The Protestant Crusade. New York:
      Macmillian, 1938.

Blanshard, Paul. American Freedom and Catholic Power.
      Boston: Beacon Press, 1949.

_____. God and Man in Washington. Boston: Beacon Press,
      1960.

_____. Paul Blanshard on Vatican II. Boston: Beacon
      Press, 1966.

_____. Personal and Confidential. Boston: Beacon Press,
      1973.

Broderick, Francis L. Right Reverend New Dealer, John A.
      Ryan. New York: Macmillian, 1963.

Brown, Peter G. and Douglas Mac Lean, eds. Human Rights and
      U.S. Foreign Policy. Lexington, Massachusetts: Lexington
      Books, 1979.

Brownlie, Ian. Basic Documents on Human Rights. Oxford:
      Clarendon Press, 1971.

Buckley, William F. and Brent Bozell. Mc Carthy and His
      Enemies. Chicago: Regnery Company, 1954.

Buergenthal, Thomas, ed. Human Rights, International Law and the Helsinki Accords. Montclair, New Jersey: Allanheld, Osmun Universal Books, 1977.

Bull, George. Vatican Politics at the Second Vatican Council 1962-1965. New York: Oxford University Press, 1966.

Carey, John. U.N. Protection of Civil and Political Rights. New York: Syracuse University Press, 1970.

Cianfarra, Camille M. The Vatican and the Kremlin. New York: E.P. Dutton, 1950.

Claude, Richard P. Comparative Human Rights. Baltimore: Johns Hopkins University Press, 1976.

Cogley, John, ed. Religion in America. New York: Meridian, 1958.

Colonnese, Louis, ed. Human Rights and the Liberation of Man in the Americas. Notre Dame, Indiana: University of Notre Dame Press, 1970.

Connell, Francis J. Morals in Politics and Professions. Westminister, Maryland: Newman Bookshop, 1946.

Costello, Gerald M. Mission to Latin America. Maryknoll, New York: Orbis Books, 1979.

Crosby, Donald F. God, Church and Flag. Senator Joseph R. Mc Carthy and the Catholic Church 1950-1957. Chapel Hill, North Carolina: University of North Carolina Press, 1978.

Cross, Robert D. The Emergence of Liberal Catholicism in America. Cambridge: Harvard University Press, 1958.

Curry, Lerond. Protestant-Catholic Relations in America. World War I Through Vatican II. Lexington, Kentucky: University of Kentucky Press, 1972.

Davis, Francis H., ed. A Catholic Dictionary of Theology. Vol. II. London: Fakenham and Reading, 1967.

De Albornoz, Carillo. Roman Catholicism and Religious Liberty. Geneva: The World Council of Churches, 1959.

De Soras, Alfred. International Morality. New York: Hawthorne Books, 1963.

Dohen, Dorothy. Nationalism and American Catholicism. New York: Sheed and Ward, 1967.

Dominguez, Jorge; Rodley, Nigel; Wood; Bryce; and Richard
     Falk. Enhancing Global Human Rights. New York:
     Mc Graw-Hill, 1978.

Drinan, Robert F. Religion, the Courts and Public Policy.
     New York: Mc Graw-Hill, 1963.

Drost, P.N. Human Rights as Legal Rights. Leiden,
     Netherlands: Sijthoff, 1951.

Ebersole, Luke. Church Lobbying in the Nation's Capital.
     New York: Macmillian, 1951.

Ehler, Sidney Z., and John B. Morall, trans. and eds.
     Church and State Through the Centuries. Westminister,
     Maryland: Newman Press, 1954.

Ellis, John Tracey. Documents of American Catholic History.
     Milwaukee, Wisconsin: Bruce Publishing Company, 1961.

Fagen, Richard R., and Wayne A. Carnebus. Political Power
     in Latin America: Seven Confrontations. Englewood
     Cliffs, New Jersey: Prentice Hall, 1970.

Flynn, George Q. American Catholics and the Roosevelt
     Presidency. Lexington, Kentucky: University of
     Kentucky Press, 1968.

_____. Roosevelt and Romanism. Catholics and American
     Diplomacy 1937-1945. Westport, Connecticut: Greenwood
     Press, 1976.

Forell, George W. and William H. Lazareth, eds. Human Rights:
     Rhetoric or Reality. Philadelphia: Fortress Press, 1978.

Franciscan Clerics of the Holy Name. National Catholic
     Almanac. 1944, 1946, 1947, 1948, 1949 and 1951.
     Paterson, New Jersey: St. Anthony's Guild.

Frankel, Charles. Human Rights and Foreign Policy. New York:
     New York Foreign Policy Association, 1978.

Freeland, Richard M. The Truman Doctrine and the Origins of
     Mc Carthyism. New York: Alfred A. Knopf, 1972.

Freemantle, Anne, ed. The Papal Encyclicals in Their
     Historical Context. New York: G.P. Putnam's Sons, 1956.

Fuchs, Lawrence H. John F. Kennedy and American Catholicism.
     New York: Meredith Press, 1967.

Gannon, Robert. The Cardinal Spellman Story. Garden City,
    New York: Doubleday, 1962.

Gargen, Edward T., ed. Leo XIII and the Modern World.
    New York: Sheed and Ward, 1961.

Gearty, Patrick. The Economic Thought of Monsignor John
    A. Ryan. Washington: Catholic University Press, 1953.

Gilson, Etienne, ed. The Church Speaks to the Modern
    World. The Social Teachings of Leo XIII. Garden City,
    New York: Doubleday, 1954.

Glaser, Kurt and Stefan Possony. Victims of Politics: The
    State of Human Rights. New York: Columbia University
    Press, 1979.

Goldman, Eric. The Crucial Decade--And After. America
    1945-60. New York: Alfred A. Knopf, 1965.

Greeley, Andrew M. The American Catholic. New York:
    Basic Books, 1977.

Guerry, Emile. The Popes and World Government. Baltimore:
    Helicon, 1964.

Gurian, Waldemar and M.A. Fitzsimmons, eds. The Catholic
    Church in World Affairs. Notre Dame, Indiana: University
    of Notre Dame Press, 1954.

Haas, Ernst B. Human Rights and International Action.
    Stanford, California: Standord University Press, 1970.

Hanna, Mary. Catholics and American Politics. Cambridge,
    Massachusetts: Harvard University Press, 1979.

Henkin, Louis. The Rights of Man Today. Boulder, Colorado:
    Westview Press, 1978.

Herberg, Will. Protestant-Catholic-Jew. Garden City,
    New York: Doubleday, 1955.

Hodges, Donald C. The Latin American Revolution. New York:
    William Morrow and Company, 1974.

Hollis, Christopher. The Achievements of Vatican II. New
    York: Hawthorn Books, 1967.

Horowitz, Irving Louis, De Castro; Josue; and John Gerassi,
    eds. Latin American Radicalism. New York: Random
    House, 1969.

Johnasen, Robert. The National Interest and the Human
    Interest. Princeton, New Jersey: Princeton University
    Press, 1979.

Joyce, James Avery. The New Politics of Human Rights.
    London: Macmillian, 1978.

Kaiser, Robert B. Pope, Council and World. New York:
    Macmillian, 1963.

Kane, John T. Catholic-Protestant Conflicts in America.
    Chicago: Regnery, 1955.

Kerwin, Jerome G. Catholic Viewpoint on Church and State.
    Garden City, New York: Doubleday, 1960.

Kinzer, Donald L. An Episode in Anti-Catholicism: The
    American Protective Association. Seattle, Washington:
    University of Washington Press, 1964.

Kommers, Donald P. and Gilburt D. Loescher, eds. Human
    Rights and American Foreign Policy. Notre Dame,
    Indiana: University of Notre Dame Press, 1979.

Kung, Hans, Congar Yves, and Daniel O'Hanlon, eds. Council
    Speeches of Vatican II. Glen Rock, New Jersey:
    Paulist Press, 1964.

Lally, Francis J. The Catholic Church in a Changing America.
    Boston: Little, Brown, 1962.

Latham, Earl. The Communist Controversy in Washington.
    Cambridge, Massachusetts: Harvard University Press, 1966.

Lauterpacht, Hersh. An International Bill of the Rights of
    Man. New York: Columbia University Press, 1945.

_____. International Law and Human Rights. New York:
    Frederick A. Praeger, 1950.

Leckie, Robert. American and Catholic. New York: Doubleday,
    1970.

Lenski, Gerhard. The Religious Factor: A Sociological Study
    of Religion's Impact on Politics, Economics and Family
    Life. Garden City, New York: Doubleday, 1963.

Lui, William T. and Nathaniel J. Pallone. Catholics/U.S.A.
    Perspectives on Social Change. New York: John Wiley
    and Sons, 1970.

Love, Thomas T. John Courtney Murray. Contemporary Church-
    State Theory. Garden City, New York: Doubleday, 1965.

Mac Eoin, Gary. The Revolution Next Door, Latin America in
    the 1970's. New York: Rinehart, Winston, 1971.

Machan, Tibor R. Human Rights and Human Liberties, A
    Radical Reconstruction of the American Political Tradition.
    Chicago: Nelson-Hall, 1975.

Maritain, Jacques, ed. Human Rights. Comments and Inter-
    pretations. New York: Columbia University Press, 1949.

_____. The Things That Are Not Caesar's. Translated by
    James F. Scanlan. London: Sheed and Ward, 1930.

Marshall, Charles C. The Roman Catholic Church in the Modern
    State. New York: Dodd Mead and Company, 1928.

Mc Avoy, Thomas T. History of the Catholic Church in America.
    South Bend, Indiana: University of Notre Dame Press, 1969.

_____. Roman Catholicism and the American Way of Life.
    South Bend, Indiana: University of Notre Dame Press, 1960.

Miller, John H., ed. Vatican II, An Interfaith Appraisal.
    South Bend, Indiana: University of Notre Dame Press, 1966.

Moore, Edmund A. A Catholic Runs for President. The Campaign
    of 1928. New York: The Ronald Press, 1956.

Moskowitz, Moses. International Concern with Human Rights.
    Dobbs Ferry, New York: Oceana Publications, 1974.

_____. The Politics and Dynamics of Human Rights. Dobbs
    Ferry, New York: Oceana Publications, 1958.

Mower, Alfred Glen, Jr. The U.S., The U.N. and Human Rights:
    Eleanor Roosevelt and Jimmy Carter Eras. Westport,
    Connecticut: The Greenwood Press, 1979.

Murray, John Courtney. The Problem of Religious Freedom.
    Westminister, Maryland: The Newman Press, 1965.

_____. We Hold These Truths. New York: Sheed and Ward,
    1960.

Myers, Gustavus. History of Bigotry in the U.S. New York:
    Random House, 1943.

Newberg, Paula. U.S. Foreign Policy and Human Rights. New York: The New York University Press, 1979.

Nichols, Peter. The Politics of the Vatican. Washington: Frederick A. Praeger, 1968.

Novak, Michael. A New Generation, American and Catholic. New York: Herder and Herder, 1964.

_____. The Open Church. New York: Macmillian, 1964.

O'Brien, David J. American Catholics and Social Reform. The New Deal Years. New York: The Oxford University Press, 1968.

_____. Renewal of American Catholicism. New York: The Oxford University Press, 1972.

O'Connor, John. The People Versus Rome. New York: Random House, 1966.

Odegard, Peter H. Pressure Politics; The Story of the Anti-Saloon League. New York: Octagon Books, 1966.

_____. Religion and Politics. New Brunswick, New Jersey: Oceana Publications, 1960.

O'Neil, James. Catholicism and American Freedom. New York: Harper and Brothers, 1952.

Pelotte, Donald. John Courtney Murray. Theologian in Conflict. Ramsey, New Jersey: Paulist Press, 1975.

Pontifical Commission of Justice and Peace. The Church and Human Rights. Vatican City, Rome: The Commission, 1975.

Pope John XXIII. The Encyclicals of Pope John. Washington: The National Catholic Welfare Conference, n.d.

Powers, Francis J. Papal Pronouncements on the Political Order. Westminister, Maryland: The Newman Press, 1952.

Rankin, Charles, ed. The Pope Speaks. The Words of Pius XII. New York: Harcourt Brace, 1940.

Rommen, Heinrich. The State in Catholic Thought. St. Louis, Missouri: Herder and Herder, 1945.

Rubin, Barry M., and Elizabeth P. Spiro. Human Rights and U.S. Foreign Policy. Boulder, Colorado: Westview, 1979.

Ryan, John A. A Living Wage. New York: Macmillian, 1906.

_____ and Francis J. Boland. Catholic Principles of Politics. New York: Macmillian, 1940.

_____ and Moorhouse F.X. Millar, S.J. The State and the Church. New York: Macmillian, 1922.

Said, Abdul Aziz, ed. Human Rights and World Order. New Brunswick, New Jersey: Transaction Books, 1978.

Salinger, Pierre. With Kennedy. Garden City, New York: Doubleday, 1966.

Schlesinger, Arthur. A Thousand Days. Boston: Houghton Mifflin, 1965.

Schmidt, Karl M., ed. The Roman Catholic Church in Modern Latin America. New York: Alfred A. Knopf, 1972.

Schneider, Nicholas A. The Religious Views of President John F. Kennedy. St. Louis, Missouri: Herder and Herder, 1965.

Shields, Currin V. Democracy and Catholicism in America. New York: Mc Graw-Hill, 1958.

Sigmund, Paul E. Models of Political Change in Latin America. New York: Frederick A. Praeger, 1970.

Smith, Alfred E. Campaign Addresses of Gov. Alfred E. Smith, 1928. Washington: The Democratic National Committee, 1929.

Smith, Donald E. Religion and Political Development. Boston: Little, Brown, 1970.

Sohn, Louis and Thomas Buergenthal. International Protection of Human Rights. Indianapolis: Bobbs-Merrill, 1973.

Sorenson, Theordore. Kennedy. New York: Harper and Row, 1965.

Tavard, George H. The Catholic Approach to Protestantism. New York: Harpers and Brothers, 1955.

Tomasek, Robert D. Latin American Politics. New York: Doubleday, 1970.

Truman, David B. The Governmental Process. New York: Alfred Knopf, 1965.

Turner, Frederick C. Catholicism and Political Development
in Latin America. Chapel Hill, North Carolina:
University of North Carolina Press, 1971.

Van Asbeck, Baron Frederick M. The Universal Declaration of
Human Rights and Its Predecessors. Leiden, The
Netherlands: E.J. Brill, 1949.

Van Dyke, Vernon. Human Rights, The United States and World
Community. New York: The Oxford University Press, 1970.

Wakin, Edward and Joseph F. Scheuer. The De-Romanization of
the American Catholic Church. New York: Macmillian, 1966.

Wartime Correspondence Between President Roosevelt and Pope
Pius XII. New York: Macmillian, 1947.

White, Theodore H. The Making of the President, 1960. New
York: Atheneum, 1961.

Wynne, John J., ed. The Great Encyclical Letters of Pope Leo
XIII. New York: Benzinger Brothers, 1903.

Yzermans, Vincent A. American Participation in the Second
Vatican Council. New York: Sheed and Ward, 1967.

B. ARTICLES

"Appeal to Brazilian President". IDOC, January 29, 1972,
pp. 43-44.

"Archbishop Defines New Bigotry". Christian Century, October
22, 1947, p. 1260.

Bernardin, Joseph. "Text of the Dismissal of Father Colonnese".
IDOC, October 20, 1971, pp. 28-29.

"Bishops Denounce Red Persecutions". New York Times, 21 November
1953, p. 14.

Blanshard, Paul. "The Roman Catholic Church and Education".
Nation, November 15, 1947, pp. 525-528.

Bricker, John. "The Bricker Amendment: Treaty Law vs.
Domestic Constitutional Law". Notre Dame Lawyer 29
(August 1954): 529-550.

Briggs, Kenneth A. "Catholics Weigh Proposals to Alter Policies
of Church". New York Times, 22 October 1976, p. 12.

"CAIP on Human Rights". America, May 18, 1946, pp. 134-135.

"Camara Asks Attention to Human Rights Issues". National Catholic Reporter, December 231, 1973, p. 5.

"Camara Charges Right Wingers Lynched Pererira Neto". New York Times, 29 May 1969, p. 1.

Camara, Dom Helder. "Violence of the Peaceful". IDOC, January 30, 1971, pp. 42-46.

_____. "Human Rights". Tablet, October 2, 1975, pp. 229, 1046-7.

Catholic Association for International Peace. "Response to the Bricker Resolution". Catholic Mind, July 1953, pp. 447-448.

"Catholic Bishops Extol Martyred". New York Times, 19 November 1951, p. 10.

"Catholic Bishops Hit Power Politics". New York Times, 18 November 1945, p. 1 and 28.

"Catholics Confirm Torture of Priests". Washington Post, 24 October 1970, p. 9.

"Catholics in Chest Fund". New York Times, 28 June 1943, p. 12.

"Catholics, Non-Catholics and Senator Mc Carthy". Commonweal, April 2, 1954, p. 639.

"Catholic Relief Aid Tells of Activities". New York Times, 19 August 1946, p. 25.

Cecil, Andrew. "Human Rights--Selective Application, Danger of Self Righteousness." Vital Speeches, September 1, 1978, pp. 674-678.

"Churches Ask Taylor Recall". Christian Century, May 1, 1940, p. 587.

Cianfarra, Camille. "Decree of Vatican Puts a Strict Ban of Communism. New York Times, 14 July 1949, p. 1.

Cogley, John. "Question of Method". Commonweal, March 12, 1954, p. 570.

Colonnese, Louis. "Text of Response to Dismissal". IDOC, October 20, 1971, pp. 30-31.

"Comment on the Week. Mr. Myron Taylor." America, May 18, 1946, p. 125.

"Comment on the Week. Taylor's Mission in New Light." America, April 17, 1948, p. 13.

"Community Chests Plan Joint Fund Drives." New York Times, 8 March 1943, p. 12.

Connell, Francis J. "Christ, The King of Civil Rulers." American Ecclesiastical Review CXIX (October 1948): 244-254.

_____. "Pope Leo XIII's Message to America." American Ecclesiastical Review CIX (October 1943): 249-256.

Conway, Edward. "Darling Daughter Amendment: The Bricker Amendment." America, January 23, 1954, pp. 415-417.

_____. "Straight-Jacketing the Treaty Power." America, March 14, 1953, pp. 647-649.

Della Cava, Ralph. "Brazil: the Struggle for Human Rights." Commonweal, December 19, 1975, pp. 623-624.

_____. "Torture in Brazil." Commonweal, April 24, 1970, pp. 135-141.

De Santis, Vincent P. "American Catholics and Mc Carthyism." The Catholic Historical Review II (April 1965): 1-30.

Dore, Edward. "Human Rights and the Law." Catholic Mind, August, 1946, pp. 491-506.

"End of the Road: Senator Bricker's Proposed Constitutional Amendment." Commonweal, August 7, 1953, p. 433.

Fenton, Joseph Clifford. "Teaching of Testem Benevolentiae." American Ecclesiastical Review CXXIX (August 1953): 124-133.

_____. "Teachings of the Ci Riesce." American Ecclesiastical Review CXXX (February 1954): 114-123.

_____. "The Catholic and the Church." American Ecclesiastical Review CXIII (November 1945): 377-384.

_____. "The Doctrinal Authority of Papal Encyclicals, Part I." American Ecclesiastical Review CXXI August 1949): 136-150.

_____. "Toleration and the Church-State Controversy." _American Ecclesiastical Review_ CXXX (May 1954): 330-343.

_____. "The Doctrinal Authority of Papal Encyclicals, Part II." _American Ecclesiastical Review_ CXXI (September 1949): 210-220.

_____. "The Religious Assent Due to the Teachings of Papal Encyclicals." _American Ecclesiastical Review_ CXXIII (July 1950): 59-67.

Fleming, Thomas. "Divided Shepherds of a Restive Flock." _New York Times Magazine_, 16 January 1977, pp. 9, 34-5, 37-39, 42 and 44.

"For a Hemispheric Bill of Rights." _America_, March 29, 1947, pp. 701-702.

Fountain, Charles Hillman. "The Pope and the Presidency." _Current History_, March 1928, pp. 767-778.

Fraser, Donald. "Freedom and Foreign Policy." _Foreign Policy_, Spring 1977, pp. 140-156.

Friendly, Alfred. "Pope Given Dossier Charging Torture by Brazilian Regime." _New York Times_, 2 January 1970, p. 10.

Gray, Robert. "Behind the Vatican Mission." _Christian Century_, October 19, 1949, pp. 1228-1231.

Hehir, Bryan. "Human Rights Factors in U.S. Foreign Assistance." _Origins_, May 4, 1978, pp. 729-736.

_____. "The Gospel and Human Rights in Chile." _Commentary_, January 19, 1979, pp. 15-17.

Higgins, George. "Human Rights at Belgrade." _America_, March 11, 1978, pp. 186-188.

Hinton, H.C. "Bricker Amendment." _Commonweal_, August 15, 1952, pp. 458-460.

Hovey, Graham. "Carter Pledges Aid of Up to $70 Million to Feed Cambodians." _New York Times_, 25 October 1979, p. 1.

"How Much to Give Bricker." _America_, January 30, 1954, p. 429.

"Human Rights Commission." _America_, May 11, 1946, p. 106.

"Human Rights: Responsibility of the World Community?"
Notes, Summer 1977, pp. 1-8.

Illich, Ivan. "The Seamy Side of Charity." America, January
21, 1967, pp. 88-91.

International Union of Catholic Women's Leagues. "Interesting
Statements of Contemporary Human Rights." Catholic
Action, July-August 1949, pp. 3-5.

Kaplan, Mordecai. "The Place of Religion in a Democracy."
Review of Politics, January 1948, pp. 179-192.

Keehn, Thomas. "Should the Church Lobby?" Social Action,
January 15, 1949, pp. 30-39.

La Farge, John. "World Freedom Demands Human Rights."
America, May 12, 1945, pp. 109-111.

Landis, Benson. "The Churches and Washington." Federal
Council Bulletin, December 1948, p. 5 and 14.

Lefever, Ernest. "The Trivialization of Human Rights."
Policy Review, Winter 1978, pp. 11-26.

"Legislation by Intimidation: the So-Called Bricker
Amendment." America, July 4, 1953, p. 352.

Mc Avoy, Thomas. "American Catholics and the Post War
World." Ave Maria, July 14, 1945, pp. 21-26.

Mac Chesney, Brunson. "Fallacies in the Case for the
Bricker Amendment." Notre Dame Lawyer XXIX (August
1954): 551-582.

Mc Gowan, Robert. "U.N. and Human Rights." Catholic
Action, November 1946, pp. 6-7.

Malik, Charles. "International Bill of Rights." United
Nations Bulletin, July 1, 1948, pp. 519-520.

Marshall, Charles. "An Open Letter to the Honorable
Alfred E. Smith. A Question that Needs an Answer."
Atlantic Monthly, April 1927, pp. 540-549.

Massey, Raymond. "Freemen are not Ersatz People." Survey
Mid-Monthly, September 1943, pp. 227-229.

Morison, Clayton Charles. "The Objectives of the POAU."
Christian Century, February 23, 1949, pp. 236-239.

Murray, John Courtney. "Contemporary Orientations of
    Catholic Thought on Church and State in Light of
    History." Theological Studies X (June 1949): 177-234.

_____. "For the Freedom and Transcendence of the Church."
    American Ecclesiastical Review CXXVI (January 1952):
    28-48.

_____. "Freedom of Religion I: The Ethical Problem."
    Theological Studies VI (June 1945): 229-286.

_____. "Governmental Repression of Heresy." Proceedings
    of the Third Annual Convention of the Catholic Theolo-
    gical Society of America III (1948): 26-98.

_____. "Leo XIII on Church and State: The General
    Structure of the Controversy." Theological Studies XIV
    (March 1953): 1-30.

_____. "Leo XIII: Separation of Church and State."
    Theological Studies XIV (June 1953): 145-214.

_____. "Leo XIII's Two Concepts of Government: Government
    and the Order of Culture." Theological Studies XV
    (March 1954): 1-33.

_____. "Paul Blanshard and the New Nativism." Commonweal,
    May 4, 1951, pp. 94-95.

_____. "Separation of Church and State." America,
    December 7, 1946, pp. 261-263.

_____. "Separation of Church and State: True and False
    Concepts." America, February 15, 1947, pp. 541-545.

_____. "The Problem of State Religion." Theological
    Studies XII (June 1951): 155-178.

National Catholic Welfare Conference. "Declaration of
    Rights." Catholic Mind, April 1947, pp. 193-196.

_____. "On Peace and Reconstruction." Catholic Mind,
    January 1946, pp. 1-5.

"NCWC War Relief." Commonweal, August 24, 1945, p. 462.

Novitski, Joseph. "Brazil's Bishops Score Violence."
    New York Times, 22 September 1969, p. 15.

_____. "Brazil's Urban Guerillas Take High Toll in
    Killings and Thefts." New York Times, 29 June 1970,
    p. 7.

Oxnam, G. Bromley. "Church, State and Schools." The
    Nation, January 15, 1949, pp. 67-70.

"Papal Talk Cheers Brazilian Prelate." New York Times,
    27 January 1970, p. 9.

Parke, Richard. "Cardinal Calls Mrs. Roosevelt Anti-
    Catholic on School Bill." New York Times, 23 July 1949,
    p. 1.

Parsons, Wilfred. "Declaration of Human Rights". Catholic
    Mind, March 1948, pp. 146-156.

_____. "Washington Front: The Bricker Reform." America,
    February 13, 1954, p. 497.

Payzs, Tibor. "International Bill of Human Rights." America,
    March 1, 1947, pp. 600-602.

"Persecution of Catholics Behind the Iron Curtain." Catholic
    Action, December 1951, p. 7.

"Pope Deplores Brazil Torture." Washington Post, 26 March
    1970, p. 24.

Porter, Russell. "Forty Four Nations Sign Relief Pact."
    New York Times, 10 November 1943, p. 1.

Poynter, J.W. "The Papacy and International Problems."
    Quarterly Review CCLXXXVI (January 1948): 70-82.

"Proposed Convenant on Human Rights." America, June 3, 1950,
    pp. 262-263.

Protestants and Other Americans United. "Separation of
    Church and State." Christian Century, January 21, 1948,
    pp. 79-82.

Quigley, Thomas. "Repression in Brazil." Commonweal,
    January 15, 1971, p. 366.

Raymont, Henry. "Brazil asks OAS to Act on Terror." New
    York Times, 25 June, 1970, p. 14.

_____. "Rogers, at OAS Talks, Favors Pact to Counter
    Political Terror." New York Times, 27 June 1970, p. 1.

Reisman, D. "Human Rights: Conflicts Among Our Ideals."
    Commonweal, November 11, 1977, pp. 711-715.

"Religious Freedom Article Adopted at U.N." *America*,
     June 19, 1948, p. 257.

Ryan, John A. "Church, State and Constitution." *Commonweal*,
     April 27, 1927, pp. 680-682.

_____. "The Catholic Reply to the Opposition." *Current
     History*, March 1928, pp. 778-785.

Salzburg, J. and Donald D. Young. "The Parliamentary Role
     in Implementing International Human Rights: A U.S.
     Example." *Texas International Law Journal* XII
     (1977): 251-278.

Santtamini, Marcos Arruda. "Living Freely in Brazil."
     IDOC, September 11, 1971, pp. 6-18.

Schaefer, Catherine. "Human Rights; Key to World Order."
     Social Order, September 1963, pp. 5-13.

_____. "We the Peoples and Human Rights." *Catholic
     Action*, May 1949, pp. 4-5.

Schaefer, Rita, "The United Nations and Human Rights."
     Catholic Action, July, 1948, pp. 6-7.

_____. "Lay Responsibility in the Field of Human Rights."
     Catholic Action, November 1949, pp. 8-10.

"Senator Bricker Again." *America*, April 4, 1953, pp. 7-8.

Shaw, Terri. "Bishops Hit Repression in Brazil, Chile."
     24 February 1974, p. 14.

Shea, George. "Catholic Doctrine and the Religion of the
     State." *American Ecclesiastical Review* CCXIII
     (September 1950): 161-174.

"So-Called Bricker Amendment." *America*, June 27, 1953,
     pp. 329-330.

Soligio, Antiono Alberto. "Organized Torture in Brazil."
     IDOC, June 13, 1970, pp. 2-19.

"Spellman Charges Protestant Bias." *New York Times*,
     12 June 1947, p. 1.

"Spellman Defends Use of School Buses." *New York Times*,
     12 May 1947, p. 19.

"Spellman at Loyloa Condemns Bigotry." New York Times,
     19 June 1947, p. 1.

Swope, Gerard. "Along the Firing Line." Survey Midmonthly,
     September 1943, pp. 232-234.

"Stating It Plainly: the Matter of Human Rights." America,
     April 21, 1945, p. 45.

Szulc, Tad. "U.S. Approves Sale of M-16 Rifles to Brazil
     3 Years After Request." New York Times, 4 December
     1969,

"The Cardinal Looks for Trouble." Christian Century,
     June 25, 1947, pp. 787-788.

"The Pope Condemns Torture." New York Times, 2 December 1970,
     p. 17.

"The Same Mc Carthy." Commonweal, March 26, 1954, p. 676.

"Text of Cardinal Spellman's Letter to Mrs. Roosevelt."
     New York Times, 23 July 1949, p. 26.

"Text of Mrs. Roosevelt's Articles Opposing Federal Aid to
     Education." New York Times, 23 July 1949, p. 26.

"Tolerance Misapplied." Christian Century, May 1, 1940,
     pp. 566-572.

Triggs, William. "Brazil: Bishops and Patriotism." IDOC,
     January 30, 1971, pp. 21-41.

"U.N. and Human Rights." America, June 5, 1948, pp. 214-215.

"U.N. Declaration on Human Rights." America, July 3, 1948,
     pp. 303-304.

Van Dyke, Vernon. "Human Rights and the Rights of Groups."
     American Journal of Political Science XVIII (1974):
     725-742.

"Vatican Embassy Harmful, Says World Council." Christian
     Century, April 5, 1950, p. 420.

Vecsey, George. "Action and Family Ministry Plans Adopted
     by Bishops." New York Times, 5 May 1978, p. 10.

"Voluntary Relief Expenditures." America, July 16, 1946,
     p. 292.

Weigel, Gustave. "The Church and the Democratic State."
    Thought XXVII (Summer 1952): 162-184.

Weissbrodt, David. "Human Rights Legislation and U.S.
    Foreign Policy." Georgia Journal of International and
    Comparative Law VII (1977): 231-287.

_____. "The Role of International Nongovernmental
    Organizations in the Implementation of Human Rights."
    Texas International Law Journal XII (1977): 293-320.

"Who Aids the Refugee?" New Republic, January 13, 1941,
    pp. 43-6.

Wipfler, William. "The Price of Progress in Brazil."
    Christianity and Crisis, March 16, 1970, pp. 44-48.

Zizzamia, Alba. "U.N. and Papal Design for World Government."
    Social Order, September 1963, pp. 14-24.

"Yalta and Taft: The Bricker Amendment." Commonweal,
    January 29, 1954.

    C. PAMPHLETS

"Alert." New York: Office for World Justice and Peace,
    December 1, 1977.

"Alert, Legislation for Full Employment." New York: Office
    for World Justice and Peace, February 6, 1978.

"Alert, The Panama Canal Treaties: A Justice Issue." New
    York: Office for World Justice and Peace, December 1,
    1977.

"Arms Export Policies--Ethical Choices." Washington: Office
    of International Justice and Peace, October 1978.

"Bishops Program of Reconstruction." Washington: National
    Catholic Welfare Conference, May 1950. Twentieth
    Anniversary Edition.

"Catholic Relief Services." New York: Catholic Relief
    Services, n.d.

"Education for World Justice and Peace." New York: Office
    for World Justice and Peace of the Archdiocese of
    New York, n.d.

"Human Life in Our Day, a Collective Pastoral Letter
    of the American Hierarchy." Washington: National
    Conference of Catholic Bishops, November 15, 1968.

"Human Rights Action Guide." Washington: Coalition
    for a New Foreign and Military Policy, 1978.

"Human Rights Action Guide, Shaping the Debate."
    Washington: Coalition for a New Foreign and Military
    Policy, July 1979.

"Human Rights--a Priority for Peace." Washington: Office
    of International Justice and Peace, n.d.

"Human Rights, Human Needs--An Unfinished Agenda."
    Washington: Office of International Justice and
    Peace, January 1978.

"Political Responsibility: Reflections on an Election
    Year." Washington: Administrative Board of the
    United States Catholic Conference, February 12, 1976.

Rausch, James S. "Human Rights: Reflections on a Twin
    Anniversary." Washington: United States Catholic
    Conference, October 17, 1973.

"Religious Liberty in Eastern Europe, A Test Case for
    Human Rights." Washington: National Conference of
    Catholic Bishops, May 4, 1977.

"The Church in Our Day." Washington: National Conference
    of Catholic Bishops, January 21, 1968.

"The Human Rights Covenants: Covenants Action Guide."
    Washington: Coalition for a New Foreign and Military
    Policy, n.d.

"The National Conference of Catholic Bishops and The United
    States Catholic Conference." Washington: United
    States Catholic Conference, n.d.

"U.S. Foreign Policy: A Critique from Catholic Tradition."
    Washington: United States Catholic Conference,
    January 1976.

Weigel, Gustave. "Church-State Relations: A Theological
    Consideration." Baltimore: Helicon Press, 1960.

D. UNITED STATES GOVERNMENT DOCUMENTS

U.S. Congress, House. Committee on Rules. The Ku Klux Klan. 67th Cong., 1st sess., 1921.

U.S. Congress, Senate. Senate Judiciary Committee. Constitutional Amendment Relative to Treaties and Executive Agreements. 83rd Cong., 1st sess., June 15, 1953.

U.S. Congress, House. Subcommittee on Inter-American Affairs of the Committee on Foreign Affairs. Governor Rockefeller's Report on Latin America. 91st Cong., 1st sess., 1969.

U.S. Congress, House. Subcommittee on International Organizations and Movements of the Committee on Foreign Affairs. International Protection of Human Rights, 93rd Cong., 1st sess., 1973.

U.S. Congress, House. Subcommittees on International Organizations and Movements and Inter-American Affairs of the House Foreign Affairs Committee. Human Rights in Chile (Part I), 93rd Cong., 2nd sess., 1974.

U.S. Congress, House. Subcommittees on International Organizations and Movements and Inter-American Affairs of the House Foreign Affairs Committee. Human Rights in Chile (Part II), 93rd Cong., 2nd sess., 1974.

U.S. Congress, House. Subcommittee on International Organizations and Movements of the Committee on Foreign Affairs. Human Rights in the World Community: A Call for U.S. Leadership, 93rd Cong., 2nd sess., 1974.

U.S. Congress, House. Subcommittee on International Organizations and Movements of the Committee on Foreign Affairs. Torture and Oppression in Brazil, 93rd Cong., 2nd sess., 1974.

U.S. Congress, House. Subcommittee on International Organizations and Movements of the Committee on International Relations. Human Rights in Haiti, 94th Cong., 1st sess., 1975.

U.S. Congress, House. Subcommittee on International Organizations of the Committee on International Relations. Chile: The Status of Human Rights and Its Relationship to U.S. Economic Assistance Programs, 94th Cong., 2nd sess., 1976.

U.S. Congress, House. Subcommittee on International
Organizations and Movements of the Committee on Inter-
national Relations. Human Rights in Argentina, 94th
Cong., 2nd sess., 1976.

U.S. Congress, House. Subcommittee on International
Organizations and Movements of the Committee on Inter-
national Relations. Human Rights in Nicaragua,
Guatamala and El Salvador: Implications for U.S.
Policy, 94th Cong., 2nd sess., 1976.

U.S. Congress, House. Subcommittee on International
Organizations of the Committee on International
Relations. Human Rights in Uruguay and Paraguay,
94th Cong., 2nd sess., 1976.

U.S. Department of State. Human Rights Practices in
Countries Receiving U.S. Security Assistance.
April 25, 1977.

Foreign Affairs and National Defense Division of Congressional
Research Service of the Library of Congress. Human
Rights in the International Community and in U.S. Foreign
Policy 1945-1946. July 24, 1977.

Foreign Affairs and National Defense Division of the
Congressional Research Service of the Library of Congress.
The Status of Human Rights in Selected Countries and the
U.S. Response. July 25, 1977.

U.S. Congress, House. Subcommittee on International
Organizations and Movements of the Committee on International Relations. Human Rights and U.S. Foreign
Policy: A Review of the Administration's Record,
95th Cong., 1st sess., October 25, 1977.

U.S. Congress, House. Subcommittee on International
Organizations and Movements of the Committee on Inter-
national Relations. Religious Persecution in El
Salvator, 95th Cong., 1st sess., 1977.

U.S. Congress, House. Subcommittee on International
Organizations and Inter-American Affairs of the
Committee on International Relations. The Recent
Presidential Elections in El Salvador: Implications
for U.S. Foreign Policy, 95th Cong., 1st sess., 1977.

Foreign Affairs and National Defense Division of the
Congressional Research Service of the Library of
Congress. Human Rights Conditions in Selected
Countries and the U.S. Response, July 25, 1978.

U.S. Congress, House. Subcommittee on International
    Organizations of the Committee on Foreign Affairs.
    Human Rights and U.S. Foreign Policy, 96th Cong.,
    1st sess., 1979.

U.S. Congress, Senate. Committee on Foreign Relations.
    Human Rights and U.S. Foreign Assistance, 96th Cong.,
    1st sess., 1979.

    E.   GOVERNMENTAL ARTICLES

Carter, President Jimmy. "Message to Congress on March
    17, 1977." Weekly Compilation of Presidential
    Documents XIII (1977): 405-407.

_____. "The President's Address at the University of
    Notre Dame, May 22, 1977." Weekly Compilation of
    Presidential Documents XIII (1977): 773-779.

Christopher, Warren. "Human Rights: An Important Concern
    of U.S. Foreign Policy." Department of State Bulletin,
    March 28, 1977, pp. 289-291.

"Concluding Document on Belgrade." Department of State
    Bulletin, April 1978, p. 40.

Fascell, Dante. "Human Rights: The United States at
    Belgrade." Department of State Bulletin, February 1978,
    pp. 39-41.

Roosevelt, Eleanor. "The Struggle for Human Rights."
    Department of State Bulletin, October 10, 1948,
    pp. 457-60 and 466.

Schneider, Mark. "Human Rights: Country Reports."
    Department of State Bulletin, February 1978, pp. 47-8.

"The Final Act." Department of State Bulletin, September 1,
    1975, pp. 323-349.

Vance, Cyrus. "Human Rights and Foreign Policy." Department
    of State Bulletin, May 23, 1977, pp. 505-508.

F. VATICAN SOURCES (PAPAL)

Pope Pius IX. Qui Pluribus. Syllabus of Errors. ed.
Henricus Denzinger. Enchiridion Symbolorum.
Barcelona: Herder, 1948.

Pope Leo XIII. Quod Apostolici Muneris. Inscrutabili.
Libertas Prasestantissimum. Sapientiae Christianae.
Longinque Oceani. Diuturnum. Immortale Dei and Testem
Benevolentiae. ed. John J. Wynne. The Great Encycli-
cal Letters of Pope Leo XIII. New York: Benzinger
Brother, 1903.

Pope Pius X. Pascendi Dominici Gregis. ed. Henricus
Denzinger. Enchiridion Symbolorum. Barcelona:
Herder, 1948.

Pope Benedict XV. Ad Beatissimi. Acta Apostolica Sedis
VI (1914): 565-583.

Pope Pius XI. Acerba Animi. Acta Apostolica Sedis XXIV
(1932): 321-332.

_____. Caritate Christi. Acta Apostolica Sedis XXIV
(1932): 177-194.

_____. Delectissima Nobis. Acta Apostolica Sedis XXV
(1933): 261-274.

_____. Divini Redemptoris. Acta Apostolica Sedis XXIX
(1937): 65-106.

_____. Miserentissimus Redemptor. Acta Apostolica
Sedis XX (1928): 165-178.

_____. Mit Brennender Sorge. Acta Apostolica Sedis
XXIX (1937): 145-167.

_____. Mortalium Animos. Acta Apostolica Sedis XX
(1928): 5-16.

_____. Non Abbiamo Bisogno. Acta Apostolica Sedis
XXIII (1931): 285-319.

_____. Quadrogesimo Anno. Acta Apostolica Sedis XXIII
(1931): 177-228.

Pope Pius XII. Christmas Broadcast, 1941. Acta Apostolica
Sedis XXXIV (1942): 16-19.

_____. Christmas Broadcast, 1944. *Acta Apostolica Sedis* XXXVIII (1944): 19-22.

Pope John XXIII. *Mater et Magistra*. *Acta Apostolica Sedis* LIII (1961): 401-464.

Pope Paul VI. *Octogesima Adveniens*. *Acta Apostolica Sedis* LXIII (1971): 401-441.

_____. *Populorum Progressio*. *Acta Apostolica Sedis* LIX (1967): 257-299.

G.   VATICAN SOURCES (HOLY OFFICE)

Decretum Suprema Sacra Congregatione. *Communism*. *Acta Apostolica Sedis* LXI (1949): 334.

H.   VATICAN SOURCES (SYNODS)

Sacrocanctum Concilium Oecumenicum Vaticanum II. *Christus Dominus*. *Acta Apostolica Sedis*

_____. *Dignitatis Humanae*. *Acta Apostolica Sedis* LVII (1966): 929-946.

_____. *Gaudium et Spes*. *Acta Apostolica Sedis* LVIII (1966): 1025-1120.

_____. *Lumen Gentium*. *Acta Apostolica Sedis* LVII (1965): 5-71.

_____. *Unitatis Reintegratio*. *Acta Apostolica Sedis* LVII (1965): 90-112.

Synodi Episcoporum. *De Iustitia in Mundo*. *Acta Apostolica Sedis* LXIII (1971): 923-942.

II.   UNPUBLISHED INFORMATION
      A.   INTERVIEWS

Bennett, Michael. Office of Government Liaison of the United States Catholic Conference. Interview, 4 January 1980.

Colonnese, Louis. Past Director of the Office of International Affairs of the United States Catholic Conference. Interview, 20 October 1980.

Gerety, Peter. Bishop of the Archdiocese of Newark.
    Interview, 8 February 1980.

Harkin, Thomas. Congressman from Iowa. Interview,
    18 February 1980.

Hehir, J. Byran. Director, Office of International Justice
    and Peace of the United States Catholic Conference.
    Interview, 4 January 1980.

Lister, George. Office of Human Rights and Humanitarian
    Affairs of the State Department. Interview, 19
    February 1980.

Quigley, Thomas. Latin American Specialist of the Office
    of International Justice and Peace of the United
    States Catholic Conference. Interview, 6 December
    1979.

Rengel, Patricia. Human Rights Specialist of the Office
    of International Justice and Peace of the United
    States Catholic Conference. Interviews, 6 December
    1979 and 4 January 1980.

Salzberg , John. Office of Human Rights and Humanitarian
    Affairs of the State Department. Interview,
    18 February 1980.

Wipfler, William. Director, Office of Human Rights,
    National Council of Churches. Interviews,
    14 January 1980 and 21 October 1980.

Zizzamia, Alba. Educational Specialist, Office for
    World Justice and Peace of the Archdiocese of
    New York. Interview, 24 January 1980.

B.   ORAL HISTORIES

Swanstrom, Bishop Edward. Former Director of War Relief
    Services for the American Catholic Church. Interview,
    22 May 1980.

Schaefer, Catherine. Catholic Representative to the
    San Francisco Meeting to establish the United Nations
    and Lake Success Meetings to write the Universal
    Declaration of Human Rights. Interviews, 2 May 1980
    and 11 June 1980.

C. PERSONAL CORRESPONDENCE

Mayor Donald Fraser of Minnesota to the author. March 16, 1980.

Father Louis Colonnese to the author. October 29, 1980.

Holly Burkhalter, Administrative Assistant to Congressman
Thomas Harkin, to the author. March 11, 1980.

Thomas Quigley of the United States Catholic Conference to
the author. October 28, 1980.

Bishop Edward Swanstrom of Catholic Charities to the author.
June 12, 1980.

D. LETTERS

Father Louis Colonnese, Director of International Affairs of
the United States Catholic Conference to Dr. Gabino
Fraga, President of the Inter-American Commission on
Human Rights of the Organization of American States,
June 25, 1970.

Reverend William Wipfler of the National Council of Churches
to Sr. Luis Reque, Executive Secretary of the OAS.
September 8, 1971.

Father Fred Maguire of the Office of International Affairs
of the United States Catholic Conference, and Rev.
William Wipfler to Sr. Luis Reque. February 15, 1972.

Rev. William Wipfler to Father Fred Maguire. February 18, 1972.

Dr. Amelia Augustus, Executive U.S. Director of Amnesty International to Sr. Luis Reque. October 6, 1972.

Bishop James Rausch of the National Conference of Catholic
Bishops to Secretary of State Henry Kissinger. April 7,
1976.

Paulo Evaristo Cardinal Arns to Father Bryan Hehir. October
24, 1976.

Open Letter to Congress and the State Department from the
Office of International Justice and Peace. April 4, 1977.

Bishop Joseph Bernardin of the National Council of Bishops
to President Jimmy Carter. April 7, 1977.

Bishop Francis Kelly, General Secretary of the United
     States Catholic Conference to Vice President Walter
     Mondale. April 12, 1977.

Congressman Thomas Harkin of Iowa to Father Bryan Hehir,
     Director of the Office of International Justice and
     Peace of the United Stated Catholic Conference.
     June 20, 1977.

Open Letter to Representatives from Father Bryan Hehir.
     June 20, 1977.

Father Robert Drinan, Representative from Massachusetts to
     Father Bryan Hehir. June 23, 1977.

Senator Edward Kennedy of Massachusetts and Senator Frank
     Church of Idaho to Mrs. Patricia Rengel the Human
     Rights Specialist of the Office of International
     Justice and Peace of the United States Catholic
     Conference. August 1, 1977.

Open Letter to Senators from Mrs. Patricia Rengel. August
     10, 1977.

Open Letter to Members of the House and the Senate from
     the Office of International Justice and Peace of the
     United States Catholic Conference. September 6, 1977.

Open Letter of Mrs. Patricia Rengel to the House of
     Representatives. September 30, 1977.

Congressman Thomas Harkin to the Office of International
     Justice and Peace. September 30, 1977.

Father Bryan Hehir to Secretary of State Cyrus Vance.
     November 18, 1977.

Mr. Robert W. Zimmerman, Director of East Coast Affairs
     of the State Department to Father Bryan Hehir.
     December 6, 1977.

Ambassador Jore Aja Espil to Father Bryan Hehir. December
     22, 1977.

Rev. Thomas Marti, Director of Maryknoll to Members of the
     Senate. 1977.

Ms. Patricia Derian, Undersecretary of State for Human
     Rights and Humanitarian Affairs to Mrs. Patricia Rengel.
     March 17, 1978.

Ms. Joyce Starr, White House Human Rights Advisor to
    Mrs. Patricia Rengel. July 18, 1978.

Open Letter of Father Bryan Hehir to all Senators.
    September 18, 1978.

    E.   UNPUBLISHED STATEMENTS, MEMOS, MISCELLANEOUS

"Annual Report of the Inter-American Commission on Human
    Rights for the Year 1973." Atlanta, Georgia: General
    Assembly of the Organization of American States,
    March 4, 1974.

"Department of Social Development and World Peace, Office
    of International Justice and Peace, 1979 Plans and
    Programs." Washington: Office of International
    Justice and Peace, n.d.

"Memo, Tom Quigley to Brian Hehir: re Argentine Cases."
    Washington: Office of International Justice and
    Peace, April 18, 1978.

"Notes, Special Brazil Meeting." New York: National
    Council of Churches, April 11, 1969.

"Police Repression and Torture of Political Prisoners in
    Brazil." Washington: Latin America Bureau of U.S.
    Catholic Conference, August, 1970.

Quigley, Thomas. "National Information Network on Latin
    America." Washington: Latin American Division of the
    United States Catholic Conference, 1969.

Remarks of Father Hehir to the Inter-American Commission
    on Human Rights of the OAS, April 15, 1974.

"Resolution on Case 1684 (Brazil)." Inter-American Commission
    on Human Rights, May 3, 1972.

"Resolution on Case 1684 (Brazil)." Inter-American Commission
    on Human Rights, 26 April 1973.

"Resolution on Case 1684 (Brazil)." Cali, Columbia: Inter-
    American Commission on Human Rights of the Organization
    of American States, October 24, 1973.

"Statement of Father Bryan Hehir to the Foreign Policy Sub-
    Committee of the International Affairs Working Group of
    the House of Representatives." Washington: January
    22, 1976.

"Statement on Political Repression and Terror in Brazil."
New York: Latin America Department, Division of
Overseas Ministries of the National Council of
Churches, June 5, 1970.

"Statement on Brazil." Washington: Latin American Bureau
of the Department of International Affairs, May 26, 1970.

"Summary: Legislative Activity, 1977." Washington: Office
of International Justice and Peace, January 1978.

"Terror in Brazil, A Dossier." New York: American Committee
for Information on Brazil, April 1970.

"The Church and Southern Africa. Report on a Consultation
Convened by the NCC and the USCC." Marcy, New York:
National Council of Churches, 1977.

Wipfler, William. "Justice, Liberation and Human Fulfillment
in Latin America." New York: Latin America Office of
the National Council of Churches, May 1974.

The Heritage of
American Catholicisim

DATE DUE

HIGHSMITH   #LO-45220